ULTIMATE BOOK OF FOUL & FUNNY FACTS

igloo

crazy humans

Tamerlane was a ruthless leader from southern Asia who led the Tartar warriors. He was a terrible, cruel person who killed and slaughtered thousands of people. He was known to build great pyramids of his victim's skulls.

A sneeze travels at over 100mph from your nose and mouth.

Your eyelash lasts 6 weeks before you grow a new one!

It's not true that chewing gum takes years to pass through the digestive system of a human.

Attila the Hun was a famous warrior in 444. His warriors, to make themselves look more frightening would cut and scar their faces with sharp knives. Attila was supposed to be fond of raw human flesh and blood.

A Roman feast included foods such as peacocks, dormice, horses and crows and snails.

A human spends three years of their life on the toilet.

Wax or gum was used in the Middle Ages to fill teeth.

There are more living organisms on the skin of a human being than there are human beings on the surface of the earth.

An average person releases nearly a pint of intestinal gas by flatulence every day.

Richard III, English King, did not have a hump on his back.

Tudor Punishment : Branded with a hot iron, M for murder, V for vagrants and T for thieves.

Biliousness - Vomiting, nausea and stomach ache caused by illness or over-eating.

The body contains approximately 97,000 km of blood vessels.

Wild and Wacky Viking and Anglo-Saxon Kings - **Ethelred the ill-Advised.**

The average human bladder can hold 13 ounces of liquid.

Dust is mostly dead skin. Vile!

Robert Liston a Scottish surgeon amputated someone's limb so quickly he also amputated three of his assistant's fingers at the same time.

At feasts, Romans would eat until they were sick. They had a special room called vomitorium to be sick in. After they had been sick they went back to the feast and carried on eating.

The Romans used powdered mouse brains for toothpaste.

Humans shed an average of 600,000 particles of skin every hour; this is 1.5 pounds a year. By the age of 70 a human will have lost 105 pounds of skin.

The human body has enough fat to produce 7 bars of soap.

If human bones had no calcium they would become rubbery so you could tie them in a knot.

Three hundred million cells die in the human body every minute.

The Ancient Britain's kept human heads as trophies. Sometimes they nailed them to the walls of their houses.

A human eyeball weighs an ounce.

Blackheads - These little horrors are inflamed spots with a black centre.

White blood cells are called Leukocytes. They protect you from germs, mould, viruses and horrid bacteria.

The Colosseum in Rome could hold 50,000 people who watched fights between gladiators, slaves and wild animals that would fight each other to the death.

Your body is amazing. It can stop a cut bleeding within eight minutes. Dried blood forms a plug, which is called a clot. It's very gooey and looks like jelly.

Wild and Wacky Viking and Anglo-Saxon Kings - **King Sweyn Forkbeard.**

Astronauts are not allowed to eat beans before they go into space because farting in a spacesuit would rip it.

A man shaves off an average of one pound of whiskers in ten years.

Macrophages are feeding cells, which eat revolting debris like bacteria, and dead cells.

In Aztec times a salve was worth 100 cocoa beans.

People who live in Asia are very fond of fried grasshoppers. They are nice and crunchy when cooked!

A person generates 100 pounds of red blood cells in a lifetime.

During the First World War British soldiers who had been shot had plugs put in the bullet holes until the wound had healed.

Medieval doctors bled people by cutting them to let out blood. They thought blood caused illness and disease.

On average a person will go to the toilet 3,000 times a year.

A human and a giraffe have the same number of bones in their neck!

Medieval people never bathed at all! Stinky folk.

It takes a human 12 hours to completely digest eaten food.

It's impossible to sneeze with your eyes open.

Glands in your mouth called salivary cause you to spit.

Plasma is a yellow river that cells float about in. The liquid is mostly water that contains stuff found in wee and gases.

A human eye blinks an average of 4,200,000 times a year.

Astronauts are taller in space because gravity does not push them down.

Ear wax helps to kill germs. It can be yellow, grey or brown. What colour is yours?

Blisters - Bumps on the skin which have fluid inside which are caused by heat or friction.

Wild and Wacky Viking and Anglo-Saxon Kings - **Canute the Great.**

Tudor Punishment : Boiled alive for attempted murder.

The youngest pope was 11 years old.

Romans used urine as a disinfectant.

In Paris in 1785 the bones and skulls of the dead were moved from cemeteries and stacked in catacombs to ease the overflow of dead people.

Ancient Greek slaves had the vile job of scrapping sweat and dirt off the bodies of wealthy Greeks.

An antibiotic cure used by the Ancient Egyptians was mouldy bread.

Back pain was treated by the Victorians by encouraging mice to run up and down patient's ribs and spines.

Bundles of muscles are found all over the human body. There are 200 in the muscles of your bottom!

Fingernails grow faster than toenails.

A human brain weighs 3lbs.

It's impossible to lick your own elbow.

Green vomit is actually bile from your intestines.

Boil - A sort of abscess, which is filled with pus.

Defenders of castles in the Middle Ages would pour hot water or boiling oil on the attackers.

There are 250 million red blood cells in one drop of blood.

Leonid Stadnyk is the tallest living person at 257cm (8 feet 6 inches).

A pustule is bacteria mixed with zit matter. Nice!

You have thirteen fizzy drink cans worth of blood in your body.

Pus is caused by bacteria. Some white blood cells called phagocytes eat bacteria.

Wild and Wacky Viking and Anglo-Saxon Kings - **Edmund Ironsides.**

Red blood cells die in about two months exhausted having gone around your body 100,000 times.

Two of the most famous body-snatchers were Burke and Hare who also killed people so they could sell their bodies to surgeons. Burke was hanged in 1832 after his colleague Hare told police about him and gave evidence in court. Later Hare was blinded when chemical lime was thrown in his face.

Tapeworms are found in people's insides. The biggest one found was 72 metres long and found inside a peasant in Russia.

In 18th century London human urine and excrement was thrown out of windows and into the street.

Separate toilets for men and women were introduced at a party in Paris in 1739.

Dr Crippen was a famous poisoner who murdered his wife.

Grown up's can make two million new red blood cells every second.

Blood is heavier and thicker than water.

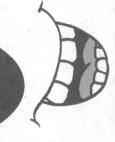

An abscess is a swelling caused by pus.

Carbuncle - A skin infection caused by bacteria which forms into a lump like a boil but bigger.

Maggots were used before antibiotics to clean out wounds full of pus. They also like rotting meat.

Sneezes are small snot particles that fly from your nose and mouth.

King Louis XIV of France owned over 400 beds!

Blood is an amazing soupy mix that contains in one small teaspoon, 25 billion red cells, 35 million white cells and a billion platelets.

Medieval dentists blamed worms in the gums for toothache.

Wild and Wacky Viking and Anglo-Saxon Kings - **Ivarr the Boneless.**

If you lay all the blood vessels in your body in a line it would go round the earth ten times.

You could cry 8 pints of tears in a year.

The Victorians invented corsets
for ladies who were ill which
gave them a shock to make
them feel better.

**Ancient
Greek boxers had
leather strips
wrapped around their
hands and some
competitors even had
metal studs fixed into
the leather.**

**Spiders webs were used
as a cure for warts in the
Middle Ages.**

On average a person
laughs five times a day.

Ancient Greek hockey players used a curve stick and a pig's bladder.

**The tongue is the strongest
muscle in the body.**

**Until 1878, when
an act of
Parliament was
introduced, no
one needed
qualifications to
pull out teeth!**

The thumbnail grows the slowest,
the middle nail fastest.

Brains look like intestines stuffed into your head.

Catarrh - The mucous membranes in the nose become inflamed causing a disgusting, horrid discharge.

Trying to stop a sneeze could blow blood vessels and start bleeding.

In Ancient China, criminals who robbed travellers had their noses cut off.

Medieval people drilled holes in people's skulls to relieve headaches or chase off evil spirits.

Marco Polo thought rhinoceroses were unicorns.

Bruising is trapped blood under the skin or nails. If it's in your eye it's a black eye!

Mervyn the Freckled ruled over his people in Wales.

Brains are quite spongy but not squishy.

Most people have about 10,000 taste buds.

Greek doctors thought that all illness was caused because there was too much blood, yellow bile, black bile and phlegm in human bodies.

The small intestine is 6 metres long.
The large intestine is 1.5 metres long.

Henry VIII's courtiers shared a toilet with 28 seats. The waste went into the rivers.

The Spartans had a repulsive soup that they gave their soldiers, which was black and made from boiled pig's blood, salt and vinegar.

In the 1950's doctors treating people who had mental health problems practiced surgery using spikes and hammers to operate on the brain.

Ancient Greek athletes who caused false starts were flogged.

If you had no tongue you would not be able to swallow.

Hiccups startwhen the diaphragm, a muscle between your stomach and lungs gets out of rhythm and goes into a mad spasm.

Gary Turner a British man can pull the skin of his neck up to meet the skin of his forehead and cover his face.

The Egyptians preserved the bodies of mummies by removing the organs. The brain was taken out of the head via the nose using a long hook.

Eyeballs are held in with muscles or they would fall out when you walked.

Pepin the Short ruled over his people in France.

Jeanne Calment died in 1997 aged 122 years old!

Spit or saliva makes food wet which makes it easier to swallow.

Saliva has special chemicals, which break down food before it reaches your stomach.

Your skin has oil on it called sebum. If you stay in water too long it gets washed off and you go all wrinkly.

Corn - A lumpy area of dead skin on the foot.

A fart is escaping gas from your bottom.

Toads do not give you warts.

To cure patient's Greek doctors would first check and have a look at your spit, sweat, vomit, wee and poo. The cure was usually leeches and bloodletting.

Aeschylus a writer met a nasty end when an eagle dropped a tortoise on his head thinking it was a boulder that would split the tortoise open. The tortoise probably survived but he didn't!

The average person loses almost a 100 strands of hair everyday.

Napoleon's surgeon was the first person to perform painless surgery. He froze the limbs of soldiers injured by fleeing from Moscow in 1812, before chopping them off.

Scientists have worked out that on average humans fart 16 times during the day.

There is nothing funny about hurting your funny bone. In fact it's not a bone at all but a nerve.

Ancient Greeks believed that when they died their souls were rowed across the River Styx by Charon a ghostly ferryman. If you couldn't pay you spent the rest of eternity wandering and wailing along the shore.

A belch or a burp is escaping gas.

Enteritis -
Inflammation of
the intestines
which results in
lots of visits to
the toilet!

**The tongue is a big muscle
covered in mucus.**

Louis the Sluggard ruled
over his people in France.

It takes 24 hours for food to go from plate to toilet.

**Tycho Braha,
a Danish
astronomer
died when his
bladder burst at
dinner.**

Misbehaving
pirates were
dipped in
the ocean
headfirst
and then
hung upside
down from
the mast to
dry in the
burning sun.

Surgeons in wars, were nicknamed
'sawbones' because that's exactly
what they did, saw off bones!

Gas (a fart) is caused by
bacteria munching through
your food.

William the Conqueror came down with an iron fist after winning the Battle of Hastings by building castles every where to keep an eye on the population and getting his barons to imprison and torture anyone who caused trouble.

Vlad Dracul was fond of hanging prisoners on a sharp pole and impaling them. They hung on the poles screaming until they died.

In Georgian Times they kept potties in the sideboard in the dining room.

Every human has a unique smell.

The acid in a human stomach can dissolve razorblades.

Romans used goat's dung and vinegar to cure leg ulcers!

Alexander the Great murdered his brother and father. He drank far to much wine, which eventually killed him.

The human nose can remember 50,000 smells.

It takes 17 muscles to smile and 43 to frown.

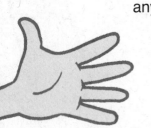

The hardest bone in the body is the jawbone.

William Sherman, a general in the United States disliked Native American Indians so much he encouraged settlers to wipe them all out.

Ancient Egyptians used animal products to make medicines, which included hippopotamus wee, and pelican droppings.

Mucus in your nose keeps germs and bacteria away. It's slimy and sticky but does a good job!

Flatulence - is when lots of gas builds up in the stomach or intestines.

Rasputin was a Russian monk who became too powerful because of his connections with the Russian royal family. He was eventually murdered by being poisoned, shot and drowned.

Tudor Punishmen: Beheading with an axe for treason or murder.

Charles the Mad ruled over his people in France.

Body waste is about 50% bacteria.

It's not possible to tickle yourself.

Warts are growths on the skin that look like small cauliflowers. A virus causes them.

Humans drink 75,000 litres in a lifetime.

Humans can live without food for a month but only a week without water.

One quarter of the brain is needed to control the eyeballs.

Ancient Greek male Olympians competed naked. It was supposed to make them run faster.

There are 100 billion nerve cells in a human brain.

Ivan the Terrible was a Russian ruler known to have killed his son and some of his wives. He enjoyed nailing hats to heads and feet to the floor.

A man in Cape Town, South Africa had surgery in 1985 to have 212 objects removed from his stomach. There were toothbrushes, razor blades and aerials! Tasty!!!

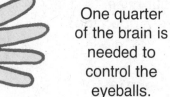

Frostbite - Occurs when bare skin, fingers and toes are exposed to freezing cold temperatures. The tissue of the skin turns black and flesh, fingers and toes fall off.

Tycho Brahe a Danish astronomer had a gold tip made for his nose, which he lost in a swordfight.

A human head contains 22 bones.

There are billions of germs in your colon and guts; they produce gas, which makes you fart.

There is a whole army of viruses and fungi in your mouth. Sounds yuk, but don't worry that's good!

Inca Indians liked their children to have domed shaped heads so they wrapped baby's heads with tight bandages so their heads became pointy.

Nits are left when the eggs of head lice hatch in your hair.

Hair loss in women is 70 hairs a day its 40 hairs a day for men.

Humans blink 15,000 times a day.

Eyeballs stay the same size from birth.

Human bones are actually beige or light brown; museum bones have been boiled so they are white.

A human's weight is two-thirds water.

Captain Cook was killed by the natives of Hawaii who not only killed him but ate him as well. His sailors were allowed to take home a few of his bones to bury.

There is a World Toilet Day which takes place on 19 November each year.

Ancient Hindi doctors soaked bodies in water in order to pull away the flesh to learn about the organs and bones.

The Belgian king, Leopold II had his soldiers plunder the African colonies of minerals and steal money. Anyone who objected or got in their way had noses, ears and hands lobbed off.

During the French Revolution, Maximilien Robespierre a French leader terrorised the people by sending over 1,200 people to the guillotine to have their heads chopped off.

Human blood is 92% water.

The human brain is 75% water.

1,000 species of bacteria live on the human body.

Every year a million tonnes of nappies are thrown away. That's a lot of poo!

Long jump athletes in Ancient Greece had to hold stone weights as they jumped forward.

There are 500,000 sweat glands in your feet, which produce a pint of sweat a day.

Gumboil - This irritating little sore is caused by tooth decay resulting in an abscess.

John Dee invented a flying beetle robot in 1543.

Louis XIV held conversations with his courtiers while sitting on the toilet.

Wiley Harp was a US robber who chopped up a boy after stealing from him. After he was caught he was hung and had his head slowly severed from his shoulders.

There are 250,000 sweat glands in your feet

There are 60 bones in the arms.

Ribs move every time you take a breath, which means they move 5 million times a year.

In the early 18th century hen's dung was put into the eyes to help bad eyesight.

Tooth decay is the most common disease on the planet.

Basil Bulgaroctonus was a Byzantine emperor who was famous for blinding his enemies.

Everyone has a distinctive tongue print just like fingerprints.

Human muscles are 75% water.

Egyptian Pharaohs had their slaves and sometimes their relatives sealed up and buried in tombs with them when they died so they could look after them in the afterlife.

A human farts an average 14 times a day.

Some Mongolian generals when they laid siege to cities fired plague victims from catapults over the battlements to infect the people with disease.

Champion long distance runners in Ancient Greece had to blow trumpets as they raced along to give the opposition a chance.

Chicken poop is supposed to be a hair-restorer.

Lice - Are found on the body or head which cause itching.

There are 32 million bacteria per inch of skin.

Francis Bacon died from a cold while stuffing a chicken with ice and trying to freeze it!

There are 6 bones in the ears.

Ladies blink twice as many times as men.

A thunderstorm can make your hair stand on end.

The Chinese invented the toothbrush in 1498. Before it was invented people picked their teeth with bones and thin sticks.

Astronauts use a toilet on the shuttle, which carries away waste matter by a rapid flow of air.

There is 1 bone in the throat.

Matthew Hopkins was an English witch finder who hanged over 400 old and weak women who he accused of being witches.

The Romans slaughtered thousands of slaves, gladiators and animals for entertainment in The Colosseum in Rome. Many slaves were ripped apart by wild animals and gladiators fought until one of them was killed.

The skin is your body's largest organ.

In the 1700's surgeons performed operations on stages in public.

Picking your nose in public was OK in the Middle Ages.

The human body has a total of 206 bones.

Henry IV, English king, insisted his knights had a bath just once in their lives.

Innuit people living in the frozen north use tundra moss instead of toilet paper.

In 1937 Amelia Earhart, famous aviator went missing in her aircraft while flying in the South Pacific.

Wild and Wacky Viking and Anglo-Saxon Kings - **Eadwig the Fair.**

Humans walk approxim ately 10,000 steps a day. In a lifetime a human can walk the equivalent of 4 times around the Earth.

The Aztecs rubbed cuts and burns with urine.

The ancient Egyptians slept on stone pillows.

Malaria - A horrid disease caused by a mosquito bite that leaves a tiny parasite in the blood.

A human thighbone is stronger than concrete.

The Spanish Inquisition tortured people on behalf of the church. They had many ways of doing this by burning and roasting them, hanging them with weights and trying to drown them.

Nerves like a giant spider web send signals around the body, which go back, and forward to the brain.

A tapeworm in a human can grow to 22 metres!

Aborigines in Australia used the moulds from under trees to treat infections and wounds.

An arthroscope looks a bit like a telescope, which looks inside the joints and bones.

Your skin can heat up and cool down so it's a bit like having your own air conditioning system.

Fat wobbles around on your bones and keeps out the cold. It also stores up sugars.

Some Mongolian generals when they laid siege to cities fired plague victims from catapults over the battlements to infect the people with disease.

Adults have around 2 square metres of skin.

The stomach is a sort of bag that collects bits of food, which it then breaks down with very strong acid.

The heart pumps away every second of every hour of every day forever! It pumps blood around the body and never stops working.

The liver is a large wobbly organ that produces bile that aids digestion and filters out harmful chemicals.

Your feet contain a quarter of the bones in your body.

Celts fought battles without any clothes on. They painted themselves with blue dye called woad.

Wild and Wacky Viking and Anglo-Saxon Kings - **Edgar the Peaceful.**

The Roman Emperor Caligula made his horse a senator.

The Maya people liked to sacrifice their victims by holding them down cutting open their chests then plucking out their heart, which would still be beating before butchering and eating them.

There are about 100,000 hairs on your head.

Bizarre cures for illness in Tudor England - gout was cured by mixing boiled worms, pigs marrow and a red-haired dog in a pot and making a poultice.

The lungs are like two sponges that store up air and allow the body to breathe.

Space toilets separate solid and liquid waste. Solids are compressed and remain on-board the shuttle until it lands. Liquids are released into space.

Parasites - Organisms that spread diseases and live on other creatures.

The heart pumps 10,000 litres of blood in one day.

Richard Dadd the famous painter murdered his father.

Children were often employed as chimney sweeps working more than eight hours a day climbing up sooty hot chimneys. Many died of lung disease.

The hanging Judge Jeffreys hung over 150 highway robbers with many bodies hung in a metal cage to rot as a warning to others.

Human hair can live for anything between 3 to 7 years.

Gases trapped in your stomach swish and squeeze their way around the food as the stomach digests it before sending it down to the intestines.

Wrinkly skin is caused by water seeping under the skin and making it wobbly and waterlogged.

Blood contains plasma, which is a yellow liquid packed with minerals and molecules.

Wild and Wacky Viking and Anglo-Saxon Kings - **Edward the Martyr.**

Pus - Not your cuddly pet but a nasty yellow fluid produced by the body found in a carbuncle or abscess.

Native American Indians used beaver teeth for knives, as they were so sharp.

Plastic surgeons can 'graft' skin onto bodies that have been burned or damaged.

Gum was chewed by ancient humans as far back as 7,000 BC.

The top outer layer of skin is only 1mm thick.

Anne Greene was hanged for a crime and her body was then sent to be dissected. She started moaning on the dissection table and was fully revived by the students.

In 1740, William Duell was hanged for murder at Tyburn, which he survived, having woken up on a dissection table. He was then transported to Australia.

Caravaggio the painter killed a man and had to make a quick get-a-way from Rome.

Bizarre cures for illness in Tudor England - wear a donkey skin for rheumatism.

The Gluteus maximus is another name for your bottom!

Bizarre cures for illness in Tudor England - hare gall and fox grease mixed together, warmed and put in the ear was supposed to help deafness.

Faeces, or poop is made up mostly of water with the rest being food your body can't digest and germs.

On the body, the hair is the fastest growing tissue.

A hair is as strong as a length of wire.

The epiglottis is a flap of tissue found at the back of the throat, which stops food sliding down into the lungs and other places where it shouldn't be!

Ear wax is a waxy gooey mass that cleans and lubricates the ear and protects it from germs.

Broken or fractured bones mend themselves once they have been put together again.

Mr Bean was the first person to take a driving test in the UK in 1935.

Ringworm - A fungus infection found on the skin caused by bacteria or dirt.

Wild and Wacky Viking and Anglo-Saxon Kings - **Hakon the Good.**

Chocolate was a currency used by the Ancient Mayans.

Woodlice were swallowed by humans in the Victorian period to cure illness.

There are 2.6 million sweat glands on the skin.

When Napoleon died his hair was shaved off and given as souvenirs and other bits of him such as his heart and intestines were bottled up and given away.

Oliver Cromwell had his brain removed when he died and then he was buried. However, sometime later he was dug up and his body hung up at Tyburn and his head was stuck on a pole for over twenty years.

There are approximately 16,000 million brain cells in the brain.

The toilet on the shuttle has straps and bars over the thighs so astronauts do not fly off into the air mid-go!

Elizabethan ladies were fond of wearing white lead-based face make-up, which unfortunately for them ate into their faces.

Just like a real drum the one in your ear vibrates when sound hits it.

The bladder is like a deflated balloon until it fills up with urine (wee) then it looks like a water balloon.

Smelly feet are caused by shoes and socks and not by feet.

A human breathes over 23,000 times every hour.

Blisters are squishy inside because they fill up with liquid that blood cells float in so they can repair skin damage.

Sweat is a weaker version of wee, which leaks through the pores!

Some people drink urine (wee) because they believe it is good for them.

Romans went bobbing for apples at their harvest festivals.

European immigrants introduced Halloween to North America by telling ghost stories around bonfires.

Children have far more taste buds than adults.

Wild and Wacky Viking and Anglo-Saxon Kings - **Harold Harefoot.**

Roundworm - A wriggly parasite found in the intestines.

The eyelid is the fastest moving muscle.

Dick Turpin the highwayman was a violent criminal who robbed and murdered his victims. He was hanged in York for horse rustling.

Sir Thomas More had his head chopped off by Henry VIII, boiled and stuck on a pole on London Bridge.

It takes 60 seconds for one blood cell to go around the body.

The brain is made up of 60% white matter and 40% grey matter.

Salt in our tears prevents our eyes from freezing in really cold weather.

Blackbeard (Edward Teach) met his end by walking into a trap. He died from 20 sword cuts and five gun shot wounds. His head was hacked off and hung from the rigging.

In the 10th century back pain was treated with smoked goats hair.

Bizarre cures for illness in Tudor England - baldness was supposedly cured by rubbing fox grease on the head.

The brain uses a fifth of all your blood.

Wild and Wacky Viking and Anglo-Saxon Kings - **Valdemar the Victorious.**

Fresh urine has no bacteria, nasty bacteria only move in when it has been exposed to the air for a while.

Cuts and wounds infected with maggots heal much quicker and stop the spread of gangrene.

More germs are transferred by shaking hands than kissing.

Scabies - Itchy flaky skin caused by a parasite.

Today, 6,000 languages are spoken in the world.

Percy Shaw an Englishman invented 'Cats Eyes' for the road in 1934.

Ligaments, which are strong cords, hold your bones together over the joints.

Females have more taste buds than males.

Over 100,000 people were killed in Europe during the 16th and 17th centuries accused of being witches.

Punishment on naval ships in the 18th century involved flogging with the cat-o'-nine-tails whip and hanging.

The hands of surgeons in Ancient Egypt were cut off if their patients died.

There are 100,000 miles of blood vessels in the human brain.

Astronauts use adult nappies on space walks and during take-off and landing.

Your nails would be 2.5cm long if you didn't cut them for a year.

In the 10th century baldness was treated with the ashes of burnt bees.

Tears spread all around your eyeballs when you blink.

Fingernails and hair are made from the same substance.

Scurvy - A disease suffered greatly by sailors in the 19th century caused by the lack of vitamin C, which causes dizziness and bleeding swollen gums.

Humans eat approximately eight spiders in their lifetime while asleep.

When Oscar Wilde was a toddler his Mother dressed him as a girl.

Bile is a greenish-yellowish acid fluid made in the liver. The average human produces one litre a day.

For centuries doctors blamed diseases on revolting and disgusting smells.

The brain of an elephant is six times the size of a human brain.

When you have eaten a meal, your gallbladder squeezes bile into the small intestine where it breaks down fat in food.

Wild and Wacky Viking and Anglo-Saxon Kings - **Valdemar the Great.**

Everyone has a unique tongue print.

Viking 'blood brothers' cut themselves and mixed their blood together.

Mary Queen of Scots was eventually beheaded after several blows from the executioners axe.

Humans will die sooner from a lack of sleep than starvation.

Tudor Punishment: Being crushed to death with a large stone.

The small intestine, removed from the body can stretch to 22 feet.

Bizarre cures for illness in Tudor England - head lice was supposedly cured by tobacco juice.

In the 10th century a spider bite was treated with fried and crushed snails.

At three months a foetus has fingerprints.

Women blink twice as much as men.

There are approximately 1, 200 hairs on an inch of scalp.

The joints in the human body are protected by a squelchy liquid. There is also a gristly bit called the cartilage, which forms a pad on the end of the bones.

There are tiny mites that live in your eyelashes.

Snotty stuff in your nose is a trap for dust and air.

Neanderthal man's brain was bigger than ours.

Tapeworm - A nasty parasite that hooks itself to the intestines.

Wild and Wacky Viking and Anglo-Saxon Kings - Harold Goodwinson.

A sultan's wife is called a sultana.

You can turn orange if you eat to many carrots.

Brainy people have more zinc and copper in their hair.

The Vikings hunted polar bears which they ate and used the fur for clothes.

Tudor Punishment: Whipping for Stealing.

A toilet is flushed at least eight times a day.

The body weighs 40 times more than the brain.

People died an agonizing death within five days after catching the plague.

The Aztecs used raw chillies on wounds to numb the pain.

Eyebrows have about 550 hairs.

Babies have no kneecaps until they are 2 years old.

Wild and Wacky Viking and Anglo-Saxon Kings - **Magnus the Good.**

If you pick your nose and eat the bogies it is known as mucophagy.

Frank Richards an American strongman had cannonballs fired at his stomach.

Threadworms - A parasite found in the large intestine.

Tapeworms can be as small as 0.04 inches and as large as 50 feet.

Everyday you breath in thousands of your own skin flakes.

Charles the Fat was a 'Holy Roman Emperor'.

The Romans did not use toilet paper; they had a sponge on the end of a stick.

Asparagus will turn your urine bright yellow.

Tudor Punishment: Standing Pillory or sitting Stocks for petty crime where people would throw rotten eggs and food at you.

In Ancient Britain the Druids liked to offer sacrifices to the gods so they often hacked off a few heads.

When humans dream it's the brain organising all the stored knowledge.

Travel sickness is caused when the ears, eyes and other senses get confused as you bounce about in a vehicle.

A strange cure for ailments - for the common cold, put mustard and onions up your nose.

The Roman emperor Tiberius liked to break the legs of anyone who annoyed or disobeyed him.

Fruit pips go straight through your stomach and out the other end.

More people are allergic to cows milk than any other food.

Only 30% of people in the world use toilet paper.

Nose hairs are thicker on people who live in the city because of pollution.

The bacteria and bugs that make your feet smell are the same bugs that make cheese, which is why you get cheesy feet!

Wild and Wacky Viking and Anglo-Saxon Kings - **Harald Bluetooth.**

Charles the Blind was a 'Holy Roman Emperor'.

Warts - Rough, hairy growths found on the skin.

Alexander the Fierce ruled over his people in Scotland.

Stomach acid in humans could dissolve metal nails!

Bacteria were the first life forms on Earth over 3,000 million years ago.

A human spends an average of 3 years eating.

Tudor Punishment: Ducking Stool for women to see if they were witches. If they floated they were guilty and then burned at the stake, if they sank they were innocent but dead.

Claudius a Roman emperor was fond of watching criminals being tortured and flogged to death.

A Chinese emperor used the first toilet paper in 1391.

A strange cure for ailments - for toothache, tie a dead mole around your neck.

If you kiss someone for a minute it burns up 26 calories.

Saxons used pots for going to the toilet, which they then emptied, into a cesspit.

Your nostrils smell things in different ways. The right one smells pleasant smells; the left one is more accurate.

King Richard II was buried in a badly designed tomb where people could poke about inside a touch his body. Almost 400 years later someone stole his jawbone!

A sneeze can contain as many as six million viruses.

Extreme ironing has been done at over 17,800 ft on Mount Everest.

At the court of Elizabeth I, Lord Oxford farted in front of the queen and was so embarrassed he exiled himself for seven years from her court.

Wild and Wacky Viking and Anglo-Saxon Kings - **Gorm the Old.**

A sewage works rots down sewage using bacteria, which eats the poop and paper.

1,120,000 mosquito bites could drain a human body of all its blood.

If you gather up all the human urine produced in the world in one day, it would take 20 minutes to flow over Niagara Falls.

Spanish flu in 1919 killed 22 million people worldwide.

Geophagia is a compulsive urge to eat soil.

Astronauts who snore on earth do not snore in space!

In 1858 there was a heat wave, which caused the 'big stink', due to sewage, dead animals and horse manure being dumped into the River Thames.

According to Viking legends the first male and female were born from a giant's armpit.

Everytime you lick a stamp you are gaining 1/10 of a calorie.

The liquid from coconuts can be used as blood plasma.

If you yelled for 8 years, 7 months and 6 days you would have produced enough sound energy to heat one cup of coffee.

The disease typhus is transmitted by fleas and body lice.

The Aztecs made sharp, slicing weapons from obsidian which volcanic glass.

A strange cure for ailments - for warts, dab them with dogs wee.

The human heart creates enough pressure to squirt blood 30ft!

You don't hear the sea when you put a shell to your ear, it's your blood you hear pumping around your head.

Medieval people used potties, which they emptied by throwing the contents out of the window and into the streets.

When people talk they spray hundreds of droplets of spit a minute.

Blood is made up of cells, platelets and plasma.

Cecil Walker an American swallowed eight whole sausages without chewing them in 2003.

Astronauts lose their sense of smell in space because there is no gravity. Their sinuses fill up with fluid instead.

In the reign of Elizabeth the I, there was a tax on men's beards.

Wild and Wacky Viking and Anglo-Saxon Kings - **Eirik Bloodaxe.**

Hair grows longer when the weather is warmer.

Injured Aztec warriors would have their wounds treated with salt water.

Rich people in medieval times had a small room, which had a plank of wood with a hole in it. The waste matter would go straight down to the ground or into the moat. These rooms were called garderobes, where clothes were also kept. The horrid smell kept the moths away!

Hair falls out faster in autumn.

The Vikings sacrificed dogs, horses and humans to Odin the god of war.

It's not true that your eyes can fly out when sneezing!

A strange cure for ailments - for headaches, rub cow dung on your temples.

Boys and girls make the same noise when burping, one is not louder than the other!

The Victorians believed earwigs crawled into your ear and bored into your brain.

If you suffer from Bruxism it means you grind your teeth!

Aron Ralston was trapped by rocks in a canyon in 2003. He had to break his arm before cutting it off to escape and save his own life.

The bowels are where your poo is kept until you go to the toilet.

Roman ladies wore ash on their eyelids.

The human body is busy making over a billion cells per hour.

You can use up to 150 calories an hour by banging your head against a wall. It's not recommended!

The spleen is a sort of filter cleaning the blood of bacteria and debris.

'Gong Scourers' were small boys who crawled along the drains cleaning out the royal poo!

Wild and Wacky Viking and Anglo-Saxon Kings - **Olaf the White.**

weird wildlife

Lizards can grow new tails.

Weird Cat Breeds - Australian Mist

Vampire Bats fly around looking for a sleeping creature, which it then bites. The bat has sharp razor like teeth, which pierce the skin. It then laps up the blood using it's tongue.

Emu's and Kangaroo's are unable to walk backwards.

Weird bird names - Tom-noddy

Wacky Herbs and Spices - Fireweed

The slow moving sloth spends 80% of it's life sleeping.

Adult animals - male hare - jack.

Wacky animal group names - a nest of adders.

Rat's can't be sick.

Vultures eat dead animals. They have no feathers on their head or neck so they can poke their heads into a corpse and not get blood all over themselves as they feed.

Weird fish - Snig

The tongue of a crocodile is attached to the roof of its mouth.

Weird bird names - Cushie-doo

Skunks let off a smelly odour when they are attacked or want to mark their territory. The smell is vile and disgusting.

Bats can't walk because their leg bones are so thin.

Wacky animal group names - an army of ants.

Wacky Herbs and Spices - Knapweed

Snakes do not wee!

Sheep have four stomachs.

Weird fish - Lungfish

Weird bird names -
Willy wagtail

It takes two days for a
snake to digest a frog.

Wacky Herbs and Spices - Soapwort

Snakes can see
through their eyelids.

An elephant
produces a
ton of dung
every week.

Wacky animal group names -
a cete of badgers.

Kangaroo's never break wind.

Snakes shed their skin as they grow, as do many insects and spiders.

Cows make 200 times more saliva than humans.

Adult animals - male mule - jack.

Wacky animal group names - a colony of bats.

Wacky Herbs and Spices - Wormwood

Frogs close their eyes to swallow.

Camels spit when they are angry.

Weird bird names - Scrub

Bats can live for up to 30 years.

Young birds eat food regurgitated from their mother's stomach.

Boa Constrictor snakes grab their prey with sharp teeth then they squeeze it to death before swallowing it whole.

Weird fish - Guppy

Wacky animal group names - a clowder of cats.

Weird bird names - Wonga

A giraffe has such a long tongue it can clean it's own ears.

A cat can run at 20km per hour.

Wacky Herbs and Spices - Pussytoes

The largest frog in the world is the Goliath Frog.

The African Spitting Cobra can spit venom six times before it runs out. It replaces all it's venom within a day.

Weird bird names - Peewee

Female bats only have one baby a year.

Wacky animal group names - a peep of chicks.

Vipers kill their prey by injecting their poison into the victim; this causes the victims blood to clot.

A chameleons tongue is twice the length of its body.

Weird fish - Nine-eyes

Weird and wonderful fungi - Wet rot

Cows can go upstairs but not down.

Weird bird names - Peewit

The African Boomslang snake has fangs at the back of its mouth. It has to chew the victim's flesh to inject it with venom, which is very deadly.

Rodent's teeth never stop growing.

Wacky animal group names - a bed of clams.

Adult animals - male rabbit - buck.

Weird Cat Breeds - California Spangled Cat

Weird and wonderful fungi - Yellow Rust

Elephants spend 23 hours a day eating.

A tortoise can live for up to 100 years.

The Spitting Cobra spits venom at its enemy, which blinds it and is very painful.

Weird fish - Nerka

Fleas can jump up to 30cm.

Wacky animal group names - a murder of crows.

The Gila Monster lizard, which is very poisonous, has venom glands that wash poison on to its teeth. It chews its victim's flesh causing paralysis and internal bleeding.

Weird bird names - Yucker

A mayfly only lives for one day.

Weird and wonderful fungi - Shaggy cap

Sharks can blink with both eyes.

Weird bird names - Axebird

The Stinkpot Turtle has a terrible smell, which is secreted from special glands when threatened.

Bats always turn left when leaving a cave.

Weird fish - Redbelly

Wacky animal group names - a pod of dolphins.

Frog tongues are long and very fast for catching bugs and insects.

The Horned Toad squirts blood from its eyes, which contains a chemical that is noxious to predators.

Weird and wonderful fungi - Puckfist

A group of racehorses is called a string.

Approximately 2,000 people a year are killed by crocodiles.

A Rhinoceros poos and then walks in it to mark out its territory.

Dolphins sleep with one eye open.

Adult animals - male seal - bull.

Wacky animal group names - a covey of doves.

Weird bird names - Tumbler

Cats have hairs on their tongues for lapping food, which makes them very rough.

Weird and wonderful fungi - Fuss-ball

A camel has three eyelids.

Weird bird names - Gang gang

Much is learnt about dinosaurs from their fossilised droppings.

Monitor lizards can swallow prey like squirrels whole!

Wacky animal group names - a raft of ducks.

Weird and wonderful fungi - Stinkhorn

Many animals stand in their poo or pee before moving out of their territory, so they can follow the trail back.

Toads will only eat moving prey.

Weird fish - Smear-dab

Some species of fish do fart.

Weird fish - Flattie

The chameleon has eyes that can look in two directions at once.

Pythons can swallow pigs and goats for lunch!

Wacky animal group names - a gang of elk.

Weird bird names - Morepork

A group of bears is called a sloth.

Owls vomit up the bones and fur of its victims.

Weird and wonderful fungi - Rust fungus

Elephants are unable to jump.

Adult animals - male swan - cob.

A group of foxes is called a skulk.

Weird bird names - Thickhead

Wacky animal group names - a business of ferrets.

A giraffe has no voice.

Snakes puke up bones of creatures they have eaten.

Weird Cat Breeds - Don Sphynx

Weird and wonderful fungi - Jelly fungus

Gorillas cannot swim.

Weird fish - Weakfish

The Bumble Bee Bat is the world's smallest mammal with a wingspan of 15cm.

Wolves eat their prey then regurgitate it to feed their pups.

Wacky animal group names - a school of fish.

Weird bird names - Thick-knee

The frigate bird chases other birds until they are sick then it eats the vile mess itself.

Polar bears can run at 25 miles an hour.

Weird and wonderful fungi - Witches butter

Polar bears can jump six feet in the air.

Some fish are special cleaners to other fish; they eat the dead skin and parasites off them.

Weird fish - Hogfish

Weird bird names - Wonga-wonga

A giraffe can go without water longer than a camel.

Wacky animal group names - a flamboyance of flamingos.

Rabbits eat food, then go to the toilet and eat their own poop. That was they get extra nutrients.

If you want to hard-boil an ostrich egg it will take you 40 minutes to cook it.

Weird and wonderful fungi - Wood woollyfoot

The milk of a camel does not curdle.

Piranha fish eat their prey alive ripping off the flesh of their victims within minutes.

You can get approximately 200,000 glasses of milk from one cow in its lifetime!

Adult animals - male cat - tom.

Wacky animal group names - a gaggle and skein of geese.

Electric eels can give off 1,000 volts of electricity to stun their prey, which they then eat.

Weird and strange chicken breeds - Asturian Painted Hen

The eye of an ostrich is bigger than its brain.

Weird and wonderful fungi - Sickener

The milk from a hippo is bright pink!

In Australia there is a fish called the super spitter. It gobs at passing bugs and knocks them into the water where it eats them.

Snakes can swallow prey four times larger than its head.

Weird fish - Wobegong

Wacky animal group names - a cloud of gnats.

Weird and strange chicken breeds - Buckeye Chicken

Black widow spiders eat their mate after mating.

Australian killer snails or 'cone shells' have enough venom to kill humans.

Weird and wonderful fungi - Puffball

The African Elephant is the largest land creature.

Weird fish - Hornyhead

The stonefish is the most poisonous fish on the planet. It looks like a rock with rows of poisonous spines on it's back.

The African Black Mamba snake is one of the most deadly snakes in the world. They can kill a human in a matter of minutes.

Wacky animal group names - a band of gorillas.

Weird and strange chicken breeds - Silkie Chicken

The Walking Catfish that lives in the Florida Everglades goes for a walk when the water dries up in its pond. It can breathe out of water and moves by pushing its tail along the ground.

King Cobra is the largest of the poisonous snakes at 5m long. Its venom can kill an elephant, which equals about 20 humans.

Weird and wonderful fungi - Blewits

The Polar Bear is the biggest carnivore on land.

Weird Cat Breeds - Japanese Bobtail

The box jellyfish is very poisonous with long tentacles covered in poison darts.

Adult animals - male fox - dog.

Wacky animal group names - an array of hedgehogs.

Weird and strange chicken breeds - Gingernut Ranger

Size for size the Rhinoceros Beetle is the strongest creature on Earth!

The largest living creature on Earth is the Blue Whale.

Weird and wonderful mushrooms - Penny-bun

The Goliath Beetle is the heaviest insect.

Weird fish - Shubunkin

The oldest living creature on Earth is the Madagascar Radiated Tortoise.

The world's most poisonous octopus is called the blue-ringed octopus. It spits out a deadly nerve toxin that has no known antidote.

Wacky animal group names - a brood of hens.

Weird and strange chicken breeds - Miss Pepperpot

Some lizards like Salamanders can grow new bits of their bodies like tails and eyeballs if they are attacked.

The sailfish is the fastest creature in the ocean.

Weird and wonderful fungi - Shaggymane

A rhinoceros marks it's territory with wee!

Weird and strange chicken breeds - Speckledy

The world's biggest spider is the Goliath Bird-eating spider.

It takes a sloth six days to digest food.

Weird fish - Slickhead

Wacky animal group names - a charm of hummingbirds.

The Pallas's glass snake will break its body into small pieces when attacked. The biggest bit with its head attached will wriggle off to safety.

A camel's hump contains fatty tissues, which it uses up when food is in short supply. The hump does not contain water.

The deepest living fish is the Brotulid.

A whale's brain weighs 10,000grams.

Adult animals - female badger - sow.

The most ferocious fish in the world is the Piranha fish.

Camels are great spitters managing to hit a target with 200g of phlegm.

Weird and strange chicken breeds - Leghorn

Wacky animal group names - a party of jays.

Owls have the best hearing of any creature. It can hear tiny mammals like mice and shrews scuttling about up to 20 metres away.

In the south of England 200,000 tonnes of chicken poop are burnt to supply electricity for over 10,000 homes.

Hippos don't get sunburn! They have a pink fluid, which they secrete over their skin.

A cow has four stomachs.

Weird fish - Wobbygong

Weird and strange chicken breeds - Jersey Giant

It is said that dairy cows can store up and explode 450 litres of flatulence a day.

An elephant's brain weighs 5000grams.

Wacky animal group names - a mob of kangaroos.

Dogs have more than 15 muscles in their ears, which means they can move them in a number of different directions.

By wagging their tails when they poop, hippos spread their scent about and mark their territory.

Owls have small brains and are the least intelligent of birds.

A goldfish having babies is called a twit.

Ancient Egyptians thought eating mice cured stomach problems.

Elephants can produce approximately 20kg of poop a day.

Weird and strange chicken breeds - Scots Dumpy

Wacky animal group names - a kindle of kittens.

Weird fish - Shovelnose

There is a variety of South American earthworm that is 2 metres long.

A 'flink' is twelve cows.

An eagle has eyes on the side of its head but it can still see straight ahead.

A gecko lizard can walk upside down.

Weird Cat Breeds - La Perm

A nice plate of fried mice was supposed to cure bed-wetting in ancient times.

A small prickly hedgehog's heart beats 300 times a minute.

Wacky animal group names - an exaltation of larks.

Adult animals - female cat - queen.

Weird bird names - Blue footed booby

The eyes of a donkey are set in such a way that it can see all of it's four feet at all times.

The eye of an ostrich is bigger than its brain.

Tigers have striped skin as well as fur.

World's smelliest
creatures -
Tasmanian Devil
(It's said to reek
of death).

A crocodile is
unable to stick
out its tongue
out.

Animals can explode naturally.

Wacky animal group names - a leap of leopards.

Weird bird names - Screech Owl

Elephants can't jump.

The tail of
a mouse is
as long as it's
body.

Weird Shellfish - Spoot

A mouse has a lifespan of 2 years.

The Galapagos Island finch pecks the backs of other birds and then drinks up the blood when they bleed.

Weird Shellfish - Polyp

A rhinoceros beetle can lift 850 times it's own weight.

Weird bird names - Laughing Gull

Wacky animal group names - an infestation of lice.

World's smelliest creatures - Striped Polecat - (anal glands can be smelled 1/2 mile away).

A hippopotamus can stay submerged under water for 30 minutes.

A humpback whale's call can be heard 500 miles away.

No two zebra's have the same stripy pattern.

The Amazon Vampire fish, which is only 1cm long, can get under your skin where it sucks and enjoys your blood.

The giraffe is the tallest mammal at 6.1 metres.

Wacky animal group names - a pride of lions.

World's smelliest creatures - Wolverines (also known as 'skunk bear').

Adult animals - female ferret - jill.

The smallest horse is a Falabella, which is 64cm.

The tongue of an anteater can grow up to 60cm. It can catch and eat more than 30,000 ants a day.

Weird bird names - Racquet-tailed Drongo

Alligators can't move backwards.

Vultures are only
interested in picking
the bones and flesh
of dead things.

The leopard has
the longest tail of
all the big cats.

Weird bird names - Roadrunner

Wacky animal group names - a plague of locusts.

Weird Shellfish - Cockle

**Hungry
baby robins
will eat
almost 5
metres of
earthworms
a day.**

World's smelliest creatures -
Musk Ox (smell comes from
it's urine).

**Zebra's have
striped skin as
well as fur.**

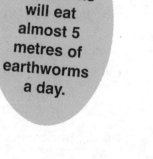

The tongue of a black bear is blue.

Frogs move food into their stomachs by using the back of their eyeballs.

A camel can wander about in the desert for 17 days without water.

Weird bird names - Northern Shoveller

Wacky animal group names - a mischief of mice.

Owls are the only creatures able to turn their heads in a circle.

It takes over 38 kilograms of bamboo to fill up a Giant Panda's stomach.

Weird Shellfish - Winkle

Hyenas will kill and eat anything they catch in minutes. They are vicious killers that hunt in packs.

A mouse has more bones in its body than a human.

Chimpanzees will attack smaller monkeys and kill them by ripping them apart.

Goats have rectangular pupils in their eyes.

Weird Cat Breeds - Maine Coon

Wacky animal group names - a troop of monkeys.

Weird bird names - Spotted Creeper

The stomach of a hippo is 3 metres long.

Cat's whiskers determine if it can squeeze through a small space.

Adult animals - female fox - vixen.

The backbone of a camel is straight.

**Weird Shellfish -
Sea-slug**

Moles have saliva
that is toxic to
paralyse earthworms.
They store their living
prey to eat later.

**The eyeball
of an ostrich
is about the
size of a
tennis ball.**

Wacky animal group names - a parliament of owls.

**Crocodiles snack on
stones to help them
dive underwater.**

Wacky wild plants -
Old Man's Beard

**A pigeon's bones
weigh less than its
feathers.**

Komodo dragons
like to dig deep
inside their victims
when eating. A
Komodo having
lunch is a pretty
grim site.

The cleanest animal down on the farm is a pig.

Weird Shellfish -
Gasteropod

Boomslang snakes from
Africa have deadly bites,
which after a short time
make their victims bleed
from every hole in their
body before they die.

**Snapping turtles are
quite fond of rotting
flesh at the bottom of
ponds and lakes and
will sniff it out.**

Wacky wild plants - Devil's Snuffbox

Wacky animal group names - a drive of oxen.

Some giant bats in Indonesia have
a wingspan of 1.8 metres.

In 1859 an
Australian farmer
let 24 rabbits go
into the wild.
There are now
approximately
300 million
rabbits!

**A female green turtle cries
as she lays her eggs, to
wash the sand from her eyes.**

Porcupines float in water.

The Boomslang snake can be born with two heads and will fight itself when eating a victim. It also has black fangs, which make it very scary indeed!

Adult animals - female goat - nanny.

The saltwater crocodile can outrun a galloping horse!

Wacky animal group names - a bed of oysters.

Wacky wild plants - Stinking Hellebore

The Goliath frog, which lives in Africa, weighs over 3 kg. Imagine that hopping towards you!

There are more dogs in Paris than there are people.

Mice do not frighten elephants!

Bulls are colour-blind.

Weird Shellfish - Periwinkle

Snakes cannot digest hair or fur but they can digest bones and teeth.

Sloths stay still for so long their coat turns green with algae.

Wacky animal group names - a pandemonium of parrots.

Wacky wild plants - Butcher's Broom

Moths that live in the coat of sloths lay their eggs in the dung the sloth leaves behind when it goes to the toilet once a week!

A frog has teeth but toads do not.

A zebra is white with black stripes.

Polecats are actually weasels.

Belching is an orang-utan's way of warning off enemies.

When a toad is attacked it squirts out a milky deadly poison.

Weird Invertebrates - Stomach Worm

Wacky animal group names - ostentation of peacocks.

Wacky wild plants - Red Hot Poker

A rhinoceros's horn is not made of bone but compacted hair.

Rhinoceroses pile up their own dung to mark out their territory.

A flying fox is really a bat.

Penguins don't fly they swim instead.

The only big cat to prey on humans is a tiger.

The giant anteater has a tongue, which is about 60cm long and is covered in prickles and sticky saliva

Adult animals - female hare - jill.

Wacky animal group names - a prickle of porcupines.

Weird Cat Breeds - Munchkin

Wacky wild plants - Twiggy Spurge

Polar bears are very persistent hunters who will go on hunting their prey until they catch it.

Crocodiles are colour blind.

A newborn baby giraffe is about 1.8 metres tall.

Elephant seals can weigh approximately 2 tonnes and grow to over 4 metres in length.

Weird Invertebrates - Bladder Worm

A baby elephant will drink 11 litres of milk a day.

Wacky animal group names - a rookery of penguins.

Wacky wild plants - Lady's Bedstraw

Arctic musk oxen charge each other when they fight crashing heads and horns.

The Komodo dragon is huge weighing in at 160kg and is 3 metres long.

Porcupines stab attackers with its quills.

Hippo sweat is red when they get upset.

Hyenas can digest bones, teeth, skin and hooves in their stomachs.

The Chilean four-eyed frog has poison glands on its back, which leaves a horrible taste in the mouth of any predator.

Weird Invertebrates - Liver Fluke

Wacky animal group names - a town of prairie dogs.

Wacky wild plants - Hairy Violet

Crocodiles cannot chew food, as its jaws are unable to move from side to side. They bite off lumps of flesh and swallow it whole.

A smelly skunk's odour can be smelt a mile away!

Just like humans, male monkeys can go bald.

Vampire bats drink two tablespoons of blood a day.

Adult animals -
female mule - ginny.

Moles such as the
star-nosed mole have
fleshy tentacles
around its nose to
feel its way about and
find food, as it is
almost blind.

A rhinoceros has
rotating ears so it
can hear sound
from any direction.

Wacky animal group names - a litter of pups.

The
Anaconda
snake gives
birth to live
young unlike
most snakes,
which lay
eggs.

Wacky wild plants -
Jacobs Ladder

Bracken Caves in
Texas, is home to 20
million bats, which fly
out every evening.

A giraffes tongue is 27 inches long.

Zebra's fight by kicking each other.

A cow produces 200 times more gas than a human.

Kangaroos wrestle and box each other until one of them is knocked down.

Weird Invertebrates - Clappy-doo

Wacky animal group names - a conspiracy of ravens.

A rat can last longer without water than a camel.

The kiwi bird has its nostrils on the end of its beak.

Wacky wild plants - Creeping Jenny

Oxpecker birds search for and eat ticks on giraffes.

Snakes are immune to their own poison.

Cows have several stomachs so they can bring their food up from one stomach re-chew it and send it to another one.

Wacky wild plants - Witches Butter

Some frogs frozen solid can thaw out and still be alive.

Wacky animal group names - a crash of rhinoceroses.

Weird Invertebrates - Clabby-doo

An iguana can stay underwater for over 25 minutes.

Giraffes sleep with their head curled and resting on their back.

An albatross can sleep while flying.

Cows have no upper teeth.

The copperhead snake, which is very poisonous, smells like a cucumber.

Scent glands on reindeer's hind toes means they can leave smelly trails for other reindeers to follow.

Wacky animal group names - a flight of seagulls.

Adult animals - female rabbit - doe.

Wacky wild plants - Shepherd's Purse

The hummingbird can hover; fly upwards, downwards or backwards.

Weird Cat Breeds - Pixie-Bob

A giraffe's heart is 2 feet long.

Cows sweat through their nose.

Armadillos are the only animals besides humans that can catch leprosy.

Wacky wild plants - Oxtongue

Cats urine glows under a backlight.

Wacky animal group names - a shiver of sharks.

Weird Invertebrates - Tube worm

A famous headless chicken called Mike lived for 18 months after a farmer chopped his head off.

The Gila Monster lizard bites its victims with sharp teeth, which have grooves for the poison to run down.

A giraffe's kick can kill a lion.

Snakes 'feel' sound waves, as they have no ears.

Fulmar birds will vomit smelly fishy bits all over you if you get to near.

The combs on chicken's heads are pieces of wobbly flesh.

Adult animals - female seal - cow.

Wacky animal group names - a wisp of snipe.

Wacky wild plants - Scabious

Vampire bats live in South America and feed on cattle and horse blood.

Giraffes only sleep for 5 - 30 minutes in 24 hours.

A polecat is not a cat.

Bats don't use their eyes to see but their ears.

Weird Invertebrates - Blubber

The stoat does a strange dance called the dance of death, which hypnotises rabbits before it strikes and kills it.

Camels have tough stomachs as they eat desert grass and thorns.

Wacky animal group names - a gang of weasels.

Wacky wild plants - Hollyhock

Vampire bats actually lick up blood from a wound rather than suck it.

The glass frog shows off its intestines and organs through its transparent stomach.

The Western Hook-nosed snake of North America farts to warn off predators.

Elephants trunks hold up to 4 litres of water.

The butcherbird of Australia will catch insects and impale them alive on thorns to eat later.

Adult animals - female sheep - ewe.

The first creatures to go up in the air were a sheep, duck and a rooster who went up in a hot air balloon in 1783!

Wacky animal group names - a pod of whales.

A duck-billed platypus has a beak like a duck, a tail like a beaver; it lays eggs like birds but suckles its babies, like a mammal. One mixed up creature!

Wacky wild plants - Monkshood

Chameleons change colour when they change feelings. An angry chameleon turns red.

Camels have flaps on their noses to keep out the sand on storms.

A giraffes tongue is pink and black.

The biggest wingspan of any bird is the wandering albatross at over 3 metres.

Sometimes cows have to be punctured by the farmer to let out trapped farts.

Wacky animal group names - a pack of wolves.

Weird Invertebrates - Sea Squirt

The Antarctic petrel will attack penguins and seals and will also rip flesh from dead creatures.

Camels keep water stored in sacks near their stomachs.

Wacky wild plants - Snapdragon

Elephants have shock absorbers in their feet made of fatty tissue.

Pigs bladders were once used as rugby balls.

Weird Cat Breeds - Skookum

At 6 centimetres long the bee hummingbird is the smallest bird.

Savi's pigmy shrew is approximately 35 millimetres long and weighs 2 grams. That's tiny!

Wacky animal group names - a crossing of zebra.

Adult animals - female swan - pen.

Emperor penguins skateboard on their own tummies when crossing ice.

The American opossum gives birth after 13 days to 25 babies!

Wacky wild plants - Touch-me-not

Turtles breathe through their bottoms.

A newborn 'Joey', (baby kangaroo) could sit in a spoon!

The algae and insects that flamingos eat turns to protein, which then turns the flamingos, feathers pink.

Weird bird names - Potoo

Weird animal homes - a bat lives in a roost.

Wacky wild plants -
Bog asphodel

A baby panda is smaller than a mouse when it's born!

The Pipistrelle bat weighs 8 grams and could fit in a walnut shell!

If an ostrich kicked a lion it would probably kill it!

Grasshoppers have white blood.

Weird bird names -
Gooney

Polar bears can smell their prey from over 15 miles away.

No reptiles live in Antarctica.

Wacky wild plants -
Forget-me-not

Wacky animal group names - a flock of sheep.

Weird animal homes -
a beaver lives in a lodge.

Female blackbirds are brown.

Giraffes give birth to babies standing up. The baby drops one or two metres to the ground as it arrives!

Bald eagles are not bald.

Adult animals -
male goose - gander.

Weird bird names -
Nandoo

There are approximately 50
million monkeys in India.

Weird animal homes - wild wasps live in a byke.

Wacky wild plants -
Love-lies-bleeding

The Suriname
Toad gives birth to
tadpoles growing
in bubbles on the
females back.
They burst out as
fully-grown little
toads.

There are
more chickens
in the world
than people.

Reindeers like bananas.

A Teledu is a Malayan Stink Badger.

Adult animals - male goat - billy.

The world's oldest crow is 118 years old.

African lion cubs are born with spots, which eventually fade.

Weird animal homes - a dove lives in a cote.

Wacky wild plants - Scarlet Pimpernel

A laboratory mouse will run five miles per night on its treadmill.

A baby kangaroo lives in a pouch.

Weird bird names - Waxeye

A rat can survive being flushed down the toilet.

Wacky Herbs and Spices - Wort

A black bear in New Jersey stole a van! It broke into the van looking for food, knocked the handbrake off and ended up at the bottom of a hill.

Snakes are true carnivores, as they do not eat anything that is not flesh.

Weird animal homes - an eagle lives in an aerie.

Adult animals - male ferret - hob.

A horse's height is measured in hands! One hand equals about four inches.

A grey squirrel that squeezed inside a bird feeder couldn't get out again after eating all the seeds because it was too fat!

Weird bird names - Babbler

Polar bears are all left-handed.

Adult animals - male badger - boar.

Frogs have an eardrum on the outside of the body behind the eye.

An otter lives in a holt.

Weird animal homes - a chicken lives in a coop.

Dogs do not have an appendix.

A mole can dig a tunnel in just one night, which can be 300 feet long.

Weird bird names - Gobbler

Wacky Herbs and Spices - Madder

Catgut is made from sheep's guts.

Weird bird names - Stinker

The longest recorded flight of a chicken is 13 seconds.

A hare lives in a form.

Adult animals - female pig - sow.

Weird animal homes - an ant lives in an anthill.

Kangaroo's can only leap when their tail touches the ground.

The soles of Polar bears feet are hairy.

Wacky Herbs and Spices - Madwort

Electric eels are blind.

The smartest dog is supposed to be a Border collie. I bet you think your dog is!

A giant tortoise can live for 200 years.

Weird animal homes - a squirrel lives in a drey.

Wacky Herbs and Spices - Feverfew

If a sheep gets stuck in a snowdrift it can survive for a few weeks.

Squirrels move home if their nest becomes infested with fleas.

There are nine sheep for every person in Australia.

Some birds can sleep while flying.

horrid history

The Aztecs only sacrificed 'perfect' people.

WOAD DYERS mixed woad, a weed with a mixture of poop and cats wee to make the blue dye.

In Tudor Times executioners killed people by hanging them or chopping off their heads.

Henry IV, English King, met a nasty end he died of leprosy.

SPITBOYS had to sit in front of huge roaring fires in Tudor kitchens turning hot, heavy spits all day.

Nasty Endings -Brutus in Julius Caesar throws himself on his sword.

Medieval Medicine: Medieval doctors could also remove bits of the body that were infectious or diseased.

Medieval Torture: Thumbscrews - for crushing fingers and thumbs.

Joan of Arc was burned alive at the stake in 1431.

A nasty Aztec death was being drowned as an offering to the gods.

Medieval EGG COLLECTORS had to climb up and down sheer cliff faces to get bird eggs. Many fell off the cliffs to their deaths or were attacked by birds.

In Victorian England, TANNERS had to de-flesh cow hides and then dip the hides into a pool which contained dog and chicken poop which was used to de-lime the hides. Can you imagine how he smelt?

Claudius I, Roman Emperor, met a nasty end, he was poisoned by mushrooms served by his wife.

Thomas A Becket, met a nasty end, four knights in Canterbury Cathedral stabbed him to death.

Medieval Torture: Iron Maiden - a sar-cophagus with metal tips on one side of the door. When the door is slowly closed it would crush and stab the victim inside.

Medieval cures for the Black Death - Cut open the swellings (buboes) on the body so the disease could escape, then add a mixture of tree resin and dried human poop.

Edward II, English King, met a nasty end; he was murdered with a red-hot poker (guess where)?

Medieval Medicine:
There were no doctors for the poor in medieval times, the barber usually pulled out teeth, set bones and performed operations.

The GROOM OF THE STOOL had to clean the royal poop pots and rear end! The groom had to collect and lay the king's poop in a dish with his hands and there was no toilet paper either!

Nasty Endings -Macbeth in Macbeth has his head cut off by Macduff.

Victorian labourers called NAVVIES had the dangerous job of building canals and railways. Many died from injuries and horrible diseases like cholera, dysentery and typhus.

In Medieval Times a FULLER, who worked with wool, had to walk up and down in vats of smelly, stinking, stale urine. The stale wee drew out the grease from the wool.

Rasputin, Russian monk, met a nasty end; he was poisoned, stabbed and thrown in the river by a group of nobles.

Inca children were sacrificed to the gods by first being given drugs, then they were killed and left on mountaintops or in caves.

Medieval Torture: Burning at the Stake - victims were tied to a stake, wood and straw piled up around them and they would be burnt alive.

Medieval Torture: Stocks - hands, feet and head were locked in the wooden stocks. If the crime was mild the victim was pelted with rotten fruit and eggs.

An ARMING SQUIRE was usually a young boy who, after a battle or joust would be expected to remove the mud, blood and excreta from the knight's armour and clean it for the next battle with sand, vinegar and urine.

LEECH COLLECTORS collected the leeches that were used in medicine in Medieval England. They were used to suck the badness out of rotting wounds.

A BARBER-SURGEON in between cutting hair would be expected to turn his hand at a bit of surgery which included urine tasting to determine a sickness and bloodletting.

Harold, English King, met a nasty end; he was killed at the Battle of Hastings, by an arrow in his eye.

Sacrificial victims of the Aztec's, after having their heart cut out and their heads chopped off had their body bits and limbs eaten by other Aztecs.

PURPLE MAKERS made their dye from vats full of shellfish, which they had to smash to bits with hammers before adding water and ash. The stinking mixture had to be stirred for days.

Medieval Medicine: Medieval doctors could set broken limbs in plaster and cover and mend wounds using old wine or egg whites.

Lady Jane Grey, proclaimed English Queen, met a nasty end; she was executed at the Tower of London.

Medieval Torture: Stoning - people were stoned for a variety of reasons and crowds would be encouraged to pelt the victim with stones and rocks.

Medieval Torture: Ears cut off - Peasants illegally hunting, particularly in Royal Parks had their ears cut off.

In Stuart Times, a SALTPETRE MAN collected buckets of urine from people's houses, which went into the making of saltpetre, which was then used to make gunpowder.

Nasty Endings - Aaron in Titus Andronicus was buried up to his neck in sand and starved to death.

Medieval Torture: Dunking Stool - used for witches to make them confess. The victim would be submerged in a river and kept underwater until they confessed, if they didn't they drowned.

NIT PICKERS were hired in Stuart Times to pick and delouse infested wigs.

Medieval Torture: Ordeal by Water - the accused was tied up and thrown into a river or lake. If you floated you were guilty!

Latimer, Ridley, Cranmer, Protestant Bishops and Archbishop, met a nasty end, they were burnt at the stake.

Abraham Lincoln, American President, met a nasty end; he was shot dead by actor John Wilkes Booth in a theatre.

Guy Fawkes, Gunpowder plotter, met a nasty end; he was hung, drawn and quartered.

In Stuart Times, a SEEKER OF THE DEAD had to examine dead bodies to see what they had died from. They had to note any unusual things such as pus-oozing boils and any other visible marks. They quite often caught something nasty!

A LEAD WHITER had to drop sheets of lead into huge vats filled with horse manure and urine. After being in the vats for months the lead had to be hammered. Lead whiters caught lead poisoning the symptoms of which were headaches, paralysis, blue gums and madness.

BATH ATTENDANTS helped people who bathed in public baths. They were expected to wade into the scummy water and sponge down a variety of disgusting and filthy bodies.

Charles I, English King, met a nasty end; he was executed by having his head chopped off.

Medieval Torture: Hands cut off - thieves had their hands cut off.

Medieval cures for the Black Death - wash a sick person in vinegar.

Anne Boleyn, wife of Henry VIII, met a nasty end; she had her head chopped off.

St. Lawrence was roasted to death on a grill by the Romans.

Medieval Torture: Strangled and burnt - women murderers were strangled and then burnt.

The PLAGUE BURIER visited houses at night and carried away the dead in a sling with a colleague. The bodies were taken to cemeteries where they were put into special pits, which contained quicklime. Plague buriers usually caught the disease and died themselves.

A LOBLOLLY BOY worked on warships and served loblolly, a porridge given to the sick seamen. He would also be expected to help the surgeon amputating limbs and them throw them overboard.

Margaret Countess of Salisbury, met a nasty end, she refused to put her head on the block so the executioner hacked her to death.

Grave robbers started stealing fresh corpses for medical schools in the late 1700's.

Nasty Endings -Desdemona in Othello smothered to death by her husband Othello.

Medieval Torture:
Gibbet - criminals were hung on gibbets and their bodies were left for the birds to peck and rot as a warning to others.

Medieval Torture:
Ordeal by Combat - knights and noblemen had to fight an accuser to save their honour. The victorious winner kept their honour; the loser had no honour and was probably dead!

Grave robbers were also known as body snatchers.

Kathryn Howard, wife of Henry VIII, met a nasty end; she had her head chopped off.

A Georgian FUR PROCESSOR cleaned animal pelts by removing any flesh, fat or gristle. Grease and salt is then rubbed into the skin to preserve it, unfortunately, they caught a number of horrible and horrid diseases from the skins.

Medieval cures for the Black Death - bodies infected with the disease were burned in pits along with their clothing.

Medieval cures for the Black Death - streets were cleared of animal and human poop and urine.

Joan of Arc, French heroine, met a nasty end; she was burnt at the stake.

Medieval cures for the Black Death - eggshells mixed with marigolds, treacle and ale and given to a sick person twice a day.

The best time for grave robbers was in the winter when bodies would stay fresh longer.

William Wallace, soldier, met a nasty end, he was hung, drawn and quartered.

Grave robbers had to dig up bodies soon after they were buried because they would decompose.

'Powder Monkeys' were young boys who had to carry barrels of gunpowder to the sailors firing cannons on 19th century warships. Limbs were lost if an explosion happened and quite often they were blown to bits.

If a body the grave robbers dug up was decomposing they would cut off bits like hands, feet and teeth to sell separately.

When the volcano Vesuvius erupted destroying Pompeii, the volcanic ash hardened around the bodies of the victims leaving a perfect body shape when the bodies decayed inside.

Nasty Endings - Hamlet's Father in Hamlet is murdered by having poison poured in his ear.

Prisoners trying to escape from Aztec cities would be stoned to death or stabbed with cactus spines.

Medieval cures for the Black Death - drinking a glass of your own urine twice a day aided recovery.

Most grave robbers drank and were drunk probably because the job was so horrible and disgusting.

In 1665 the village of Eyam in the UK contracted the plague. A delivery of cloth from London contained fleas, which carried the Black Death. They closed the village to contain the disease, which was successful. Of the 350 villagers only 84 survived.

A nasty Aztec death - skinned alive.

As there were no sewers in Gong-scourer's went into cesspits to clear out the disgusting stinking mess. They had to shovel it out into buckets during the night, as the smell was so vile. Children were used to clear out the narrow parts of the pit and scrape out the poop and wee.

Shepherd boys were left in charge of big flocks of sheep and in serious trouble if any went missing. Sometimes the sheep would fill up with gas and the shepherd boys would have to stab it in the right place in the stomach to let the smelly gas out.

Medieval cures for the Black Death - witchcraft cures suggesting putting a live hen next to the buboes to draw out the badness.

Children working on the land in medieval times had to be up before dawn feeding the animals and mucking out animal poop with shovels and handcarts.

In Victorian England horses were used as transport so there were tons of horse poop on the roads. Orderly boys had to shovel up the piles of horse poop and put it into bins.

Medieval Torture: Hung, Drawn and Quartered - those found guilty of high treason were hung, then cut down to have their intestines cut open and drawn out while they were still alive then they were finally quartered into four pieces.

Julius Caesar, Roman dictator, met a nasty end; Brutus, Cassius and others stabbed him in the Senate.

A nasty Aztec death - beheaded.

Whipping boys got hit instead of the royal person who was practicing his letters. If the royal did not complete the lesson or misbehaved the teacher would hit the whipping boy instead of the royal.

Medieval Torture: Ordeal by Fire - the accused was made to hold a red-hot iron bar and then walk three paces. The hand was then bandaged and left for three days. If the burn was better you were innocent, if the burn was no better you were guilty.

The workhouse was a terrible place and so were many of the jobs. Children were given tasks such as sewing heavy sacks until their fingers bled and picking oakum (pulling rope to pieces), which left your hands raw.

Many children were employed in factories and mills and expected to climb under and in the machinery while it was still running to clean it. Many lost limbs, their hair or were killed.

The Rack was a medieval torture instrument, which stretched the victims who were tied by their wrists and ankles.

John.F.Kennedy, American President, met a nasty end; he was shot while riding in a car in Dallas, Texas by rifleman Lee Harvey Oswald.

Coal mines used children for pushing and pulling heavy carts of coal in narrow tunnels underground. They were quite often killed or badly injured or caught horrible lung diseases from the coal dust.

Creepy Creatures

Dinosaur means 'terrible lizard'.

Blue-black spider wasps terrify there pray into submission with their loud buzz.

Praying mantis lie in wait for their victims, which they grab and hold with their spiny forelegs. They eat their prey upside-down.

Dung Beetles roll huge balls of dung, which they keep underground for food for their grubs.

Starfish can turn their stomachs inside out. Messy!

The brightly coloured poison Dart Frog has very poisonous slimy mucus.

Woodlouse-eating spiders have big jaws, which are designed to catch and crunch woodlice.

A butterfly has taste buds in its feet.

House flies live for 2 - 3 weeks.

The body of a leech will swell up considerably after they have gorged on a meal of blood, sometimes as much as 20cms. They move along with suckers, which they have at the front and back of their bodies. The front sucker is also the mouth and has teeth.

Snails and slugs sometimes attack and eat each other. An attacker will drill a hole in the other snail's shell to eat it. They slither along on trails of slime.

Sharks grow a new set of teeth every week.

Bluebottle flies can smell meat from a distance of 7km.

Giant Arctic jellyfish have poisonous tentacles, which are deadly. The tentacles can be 30 metres long.

The female mosquitoes suck blood before they lay eggs. They can suck over half a litre of human blood in an hour. The male mos-quitoes suck the juices of plants instead of blood.

The skeletons of sharks are made of cartilage instead of bones.

Mosquito's have 47 teeth.

A moth does not have a stomach.

Robber Flies have sharp mouthparts, which they use to stab their prey when they have caught it. They then suck them dry.

Only female wasps sting.

The Black widow spider spins a web to trap its prey. Once caught the spider then sucks out the victim's insides.

A cricket's ears are found below its knees.

A swarm of locusts can munch through 20,000 tons of vegetation a day.

The teeth of Tyrannosaurus were sharp, long and ideal for tearing and slicing flesh.

Tyrannosaurus was to heavy to run after prey so it grabbed slower dinosaurs or ate dead ones.

A Starfish can grow new arms if they get damaged.

Ticks are parasites, which stab animals and humans with their hooked mouthparts. They suck blood, which swells up their bodies.

Fleas, like ticks hook onto the fur and skin of animals and humans. They have large back legs which means they can jump over half a metre. Fleas can carry diseases, which they pass on to the victims they, bite. The fleas of rats, which killed millions of people, spread the Black Death in the Middle Ages.

Slow worms can re-grow the part that has been broken-off.

A Cockroach can in one year produce 30,000 young. It can also live for several weeks without a head.

A female cod is believed to lay 9 million eggs.

Snails are hermaphrodites, which means they are both male and female.

Porcupine Fish can fill themselves up with seawater and expand up so they look like a giant football. The skin and sharp spines of the fish are very poisonous.

The Lion fish is an amazingly colourful fish with deadly spines coated in a toxic mucus, which causes terrible agony.

The world's longest animal is the bootlace worm.

If you cut a worm in half only the head will live.

Fly larvae eggs are laid on dung. The larvae have no legs so they move about by wiggling through the squidgy, squelchy dung, which they also eat.

Some dinosaurs had up to 2000 teeth.

Ants crawl on birds and spray them with acid. The birds don't mind this as it gets rid of nasty parasites off their feathers.

Flies eat and lay their eggs on dead bodies. When the eggs hatch the maggots eat the rotten flesh. After eating, a fly regurgitates food and eats it again.

Cockroaches have been on earth for 300 million years. They don't seem to have changed much!

There are over 9000 different species of ants.

The Portuguese Man O'War jellyfish is a very poisonous jellyfish. Their long tentacles sting and shoot tiny prickly barbs into anything that touches them.

Paper wasps chew wood with their saliva to make paper nests.

Shieldbugs are sometimes called stinkbugs because they ooze a liquid, which stinks when they are in danger of being attacked.

Starfish have no brains.

Army ants do not live in anthills because they are nomadic. A swarm of Army ants can contain a million ants, which can eat 50,000 insects in one day - greedy lot!!

The babies of Tiger Sharks fight each other in their mother's womb; the baby shark born is the survivor.

Dung beetles were thought by the Ancient Egyptians to have been born from a ball of dung.

Some creepy crawlies and bugs have stink glands to chase off predators.

Scientists have discovered what dinosaurs ate by investigating their droppings.

Army ants eat anything that gets in their way including small creatures, birds and even horses!

The army ant queen lays millions of eggs in one month.

Sandwasps leave food for their young, sandwasps catch and sting a caterpillar into sleep; they then bury the caterpillar and lay an egg on it. When the larva hatches from the egg they eat the sleeping caterpillar.

Bees have five eyes but no ears.

The female parasitic wasp injects her eggs into the body of another insect. When the eggs hatch they eat their way out of the creature.

The sea is very dark and cold at depths of over one kilometre so strange creatures live there. The deep-sea angler fish glows faintly due to a growth over its mouth. Other fish are attracted to the light before the angler fish swallows them whole.

Weaver ants are carnivores that eat other soft-bodied insects by sucking fluids from them.

Weaver ants contain oil, which is sweet so they are considered a delicacy by Eastern cultures.

A queen leafcutter ant during her lifetime can produce 15 million young leaf-cutter ants.

There is a lot of protein in leafcutter ants so many cultures like eating them.

Bombardier beetles spray boiling poisonous fluids at their attackers.

Dinosaurs that only ate plants needed to eat a tonne of vegetation a day.

A shrimp swims backwards.

Lampreys a long eel like fish, which has a hooked circular mouth, which gnaws and nibbles into the flesh of other fish. They can wriggle through and into the bodies of the fish they are attacking.

House flies lay their eggs in household waste or animal manure.

Butterflies suck nectar with a device called a proboscis as they have no teeth or a mouth.

Female honeybees die when they sting a victim, as their insides are torn out.

Bumblebees make honey for themselves and their young not for us!

Hornets are ferocious huge wasps.

Queen bees lay 600 to 700 eggs a day.

Velvet ants are parasites and lay their eggs in bee's nests. The larva when they hatch eats the eggs and young of the bees.

Bombardier beetles like to scuttle about in rotting wood and they lay their eggs in decomposing matter.

Parasitic wasps can inject and lay up to 3000 eggs inside a single insect.

The Rhinoceros beetle has fiercesome horns that they use to pierce the bodies of other insects.

Dinosaurs had dry, tough waterproof skin made of scales.

Stegosaurs had the smallest brain, which was the size of a walnut.

Wasps have sharp jagged edges on their jaws for cutting.

Bumblebees live together in colonies. There can be anything from 40 to 600 bees.

The heart of a shrimp is in its head.

The Death's head hawk-moth takes honey from bee's nests.

Herring Fish communicate by breaking wind.

Sharks can smell a tiny droplet of blood many kilometres from their intended victim before they move in for the kill.

Red admiral butterflies like to feed on rotting fruit, bird droppings and tree sap.

The larvae of the horse fly feed on other insects but will eat each other if there is no other food.

Vinegar flies transmit germs and disease from rotten and decaying food.

Tiger beetle larvae have large jaws, which they use to catch and eat insects.

The mouth of a housefly is like a sponge, which sucks up liquid food.

House-flies have sticky pads on their legs, which let them walk upside down.

An octopus has three hearts.

The Assassin bug kills its prey by injecting the victim with venom that will paralyse the victim and start to dissolve it. The Assassin bug then sucks up the liquid from the victim.

Lobster moth larvae look like lobsters with their six wriggling legs and a swollen tail like a lobster.

The hagfish bores its way into its victims and eats them from the inside. It also creates huge amounts of slime.

The larvae and female fireflies eat slugs, snails and worms.

The Assassin bug can blind humans temporarily with its saliva.

Fireflies are a type of beetle sometimes called lightning bugs.

The mark of a skull on the Death head hawk-moth's thorax gives it its name.

Dinosaurs that were active, fast meat eaters had the largest brains.

Rhinoceros beetles feed on plant sap and rotten fruit.

Some dinosaurs used their thick bony, heavy skulls to batter their victims to death.

A seagull would explode if it drank an alka seltzer.

Female fireflies attract males by flashing their light, then they eat them!

If it is not disturbed a horse fly will suck blood for half an hour from a victim.

Diving beetles use their tough hairy legs like oars to move about.

Insects avoid eating Tiger beetles because they taste horrible!

Ladybird beetles are brightly coloured which means they taste vile!

Horse flies suck and feed on the blood of animals and humans.

Male sea horses get pregnant.

Lobsters can grow new eyeballs.

Diving beetle larvae are known as 'water tigers' because they will attack and eat small fish and tadpoles.

The bombardier beetle can squirt a poisonous spray of liquid from its abdomen.

A species of Cicada which lives under-ground only comes out into the open every seventeen years.

There was no grass at the time of the dinosaurs so they ate shrubs and small trees.

Stag beetles have strong jaws, which they use to nip and draw blood.

Spittlebugs produce a substance called 'cuckoo spit' which is sticky and frothy and protects the young bug.

Cicadas are eaten by peoples in Borneo and Malaysia.

Tiger beetles pounce on their prey and use their jaws to tear it to pieces.

Dolphins sleep with one eye open.

Stinkbugs have a sort of anti-freeze in their bodies called glycerol, which stops them freezing in winter.

Aphid bugs have large stomachs with two tubes attached to it called comicles from which they ooze wax.

If you upset a lady-bird it will release a disgusting, smelly liquid, which stains.

The eggs of a mealy bug are attached to their bodies.

Squash bugs have powerful beaks, which suck fluids out of insects.

Aphid bugs give birth to 100 young in one go.

A jellyfish is 95% water.

Sea anemones sting passing creatures with its tentacles.

Aphids are sapsuckers.

Giant water bugs are very fierce and can even hunt some fish. They have been known to bite humans who paddle in ponds. They clamp their prey in big claws and then inject them with poison that paralyses it. They then suck the victim dry!

Mealy bugs produce a sticky substance called honeydew. Ants like this and are often found with mealy bugs. Sticky friends!!

Cockroaches help the environment by eating waste including animal waste. But they can spread diseases.

The Water boatman insects are not really that good on water! If they stop swimming they sink!

A dinosaur named Euoplocephalus bashed its attackers on the head and stunned them with its bony tail.

Some tribal groups eat dried locusts.

Crickets rub their wings together to make sounds.

Many dinosaurs walked on their toes.

The female tortoise beetle keeps faeces on it's prickly back to rub in the face of any bug thinking about preying on it. Nice!

The cockroach is not a dirty bug; it's the nasty germs they pick up that infect humans.

Stinkbugs are eaten in India, Africa and Mexico.

In Mexico they dry and eat water boatman eggs.

Archer fish spit a jet of water into the air to knock insects off leaves and into their waiting jaws.

Backswimmer bugs have nasty toxins in their body, which kills other insects.

The Sea Cucumber when it is attacked fires darts covered in poison from its bum!

A giant water bug makes a tasty snack in some countries.

Katydid bugs have eardrums on their front legs.

Lobsters have blue blood.

Cockroaches are speedy bugs that move very fast.

The biggest snail ever found was an African snail that weighed 1kg and measured 40cm.

You can find cockroaches almost everywhere in most environments.

Octopuses fire an inky cloud at anything trying to attack it.

Grasshoppers spit a vile brown liquid, which protects them from insects preying on them.

Some dinosaurs fought each other to the death. Skeletons of fighting dinosaurs have been found locked together.

The female giant water bug lays eggs on the back of the male who has to take care of them until they hatch.

Backswimmer bugs have a body shaped like the bottom of a boat. It has a nasty bite and can bite humans!

The noise a Katydid makes sounds like Katy-did-Katy-didn't.

There are 1,800 known species of fleas.

Stegosaurus had armoured skin made of hard plates, horns and spikes.

Bees collect nectar and keep it in one of their stomachs where it turns into honey. The bees then vomit the honey up to make the honeycomb.

The cockroaches that live on the island of Madagascar are called Madagascar hissing cockroaches because .... they hiss!

Scallops like to see who is creeping up on them so they have 100 eyes dotted around their shells.

Stick insects can grow new legs if they lose one!

The tongue of a blue whale is the weight and size of an adult African elephant!

Dragonflies have strong jaws, which enable them to catch prey.

Water striders can run very fast across water. If they were the same size as humans they would be as fast as an aeroplane.

Brachlosaurus weighed 80 tonnes.

The Bombardier beetles when attacked covers its predators with hot burning acid.

Damselflies catch lunch by folding their legs around their prey like a basket.

Sea cucumbers will vomit the contents of their guts over their enemies.

Silverfish are primitive bugs, which are often found in kitchens or bathroom.

The dragonfly was the inspiration for the design of helicopters.

Praying mantis females eat the male while they are mating.

The Oriental cockroach can grow up to 4cm in length.

A slug has four noses.

The giant squid has the biggest eye at 40cm.

The spook-fish, which lives in the Pacific Ocean, has a snout filled with mucus for detecting electric charges.

The praying mantis grabs its prey with its long front legs before eating it.

In Australia, baby crab spiders bite off their mother's limbs to eat.

Leeches suck five times their weight in blood before they fall off their victim.

The great white shark has a mouthful of 3,000 teeth.

Silverfish have shiny scales, which gives them their name.

It's not unusual for a female dragonfly to lay 100,000 eggs in one go!

Death's head cockroaches are kept as pets.

Butterflies have 12,000 eyes!

In Australia, the duckbill platypus stores over 600 worms in its cheek pouches.

Some ants eat caterpillar droppings because they contain minerals for their diets.

A running cockroach can get up to three miles an hour.

Meat eating dinosaurs ate smaller reptiles, insects, fish and birds.

Centipedes when walking have uneven pairs of legs.

Soldier termites shoot globules of itchy glue at anything that attacks them.

Lesothosaurus was the size of a chicken.

Silkworms are really caterpillars.

A flea can jump 1metre into the air.

The lady tortoise beetle rubs its backside in the face of predators covering them with a disgusting gooey mess.

The slimebag, which is a hag-fish, produces loads of gooey slime to protect its self.

Butterflies have skeletons outside their bodies, which are called exoskeletons.

The blue whale has over 8,000 litres of blood pumping through its body.

Ribbon worms can eat themselves if they can't find food.

A number of creepy crawlies and beetles have poisonous poop.

There are thousands of bedbugs in your bed and they suck blood.

There are no ants in Iceland, Antarctica or Greenland.

A blue whale can eat 40 million krill a day!

Horseflies are bloodsuckers that give a horrid bite that can make the bitten area swell up horribly.

Fleas were responsible for spreading the disease the Black Death in medieval Europe.

Camarasaurus had nostrils on top of its head.

The queen termite is much larger than other termites approximately one hundred times longer. She's big!

The coconut crab climbs trees to pick coconuts.

The hagfish sneezes out slime from its nose after squirting it at victims.

There are 980 species of bats.

Leeches have 32 brains.

In order to swallow prey bigger than itself the angler fish has an elastic stomach.

If you like tasty foods try these, wasps taste like pine nuts, beetles taste like apples and worms taste like fried bacon.

No creature preys on the white shark, it has no natural enemies.

The South African rock scorpion can grow to 25cm in length.

Some dinosaurs killed and ate their own kind.

Millipedes have the most legs of any creature.

House dust mites like munching on dead skin.

Midges are bloodsuckers.

Dinosaurs usually laid 30 or more eggs.

The saliva from leeches is made into medicine for treating illnesses in humans.

In Africa when the drought comes the African Lungfish burrows into the mud of the river bed and covers itself with mucus that keeps it from drying out until the rains come.

A dragonfly can fly at 30 miles an hour.

The colour of your hair determines what colour the head-lice are.

The Venus flytrap plant waits for an unsuspecting fly to land on it and then snaps shut! Mm lunch!

Caterpillars can stare at you with all of their twelve eyes.

The maggots of the blowfly are used in some hospitals to clean out infected wounds.

Ants can pull 30 times their own weight.

Spider babies eat their mother when she dies.

The most pongy, smelliest plant on the planet is the Corpse lily, which grows in Cambodia. It smells like rotting flesh.

There are 10 to 1 more termites in the world than humans.

An ant can survive underwater for two days.

Fossil information shows that sharks are older than dinosaurs.

The pearl-fish lives in the bum of the sea cucumber.

Swordfish can swim at 68 miles per hour, which makes them the fastest fish in the ocean.

The Tanzanian parasitic wasp is smaller than the eye of a housefly.

Termites are an Anteaters favourite dish not ants.

Ants can lift 50 times it's own weight.

Apart from mosquitoes, ticks are the second most dangerous parasite to humans.

Millipedes roll up into a crunchy ball to escape being eaten.

Earthworms don't have eyes they have light sensors all over their bodies.

Diplodocus had the smallest brain of all the dinosaurs, which was probably the size of a pea!

Scientists have learned lots about dinosaurs by studying their droppings.

Bed bugs have a horrible smell as well as sucking blood while people sleep.

Maggots cover food with their spit to dissolve it then they suck it up.

A bedbug can survive for a year without feeding.

Spider webs are five times stronger than steel.

The tsetse fly kills 66,000 people every year.

The giant centipede, which grows to 30 cm in length, can kill mice and frogs using two pincers at the back of its head.

Octopuses kill lobsters by biting through their shell and spitting into the bite with poisonous spit.

In order to find their way around in the dark bats squeak and the echo bounces back to them.

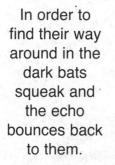

The biggest creature without a backbone is a giant squid.

The giant squid has the largest eyeballs in the world.

Flies crash into windows because they can't see the glass!

There are well over 1500 species of flea.

An electric eel can shock you with 650 volts.

Dinosaurs disappeared from Earth before the Alps or the Rocky Mountains were formed.

Midges flap their wings 1,046 times per second.

Cockroaches are super fast bugs, which can move at one metre per second.

The poison an octopus uses to kill its prey turns the creatures flesh to a pulpy sludgy mess, which the octo-pus sucks up.

Ninety nine percent of baby tarantulas are killed by their mother.

A moth larva inside a Mexican jumping bean is what makes it jump.

Dragonflies have fearsome snapping jaws.

Some spiders spit poisonous slime at their victims.

Lizards can wipe their eyeballs with their tongue.

'Woolly bears' are carpet-beetle grubs that eat their way through carpets but they are quite fond of pet and human hairs.

The Monarch Butterfly flies 3,000 kilometres when it migrates.

Fleas launch themselves like jack-in-the-boxes.

Apatosaurus could produce more than a tonne of smelly poop a day.

A female flea consumes 15 times its body weight in blood daily.

A mummy lobster can lay 50,000 eggs at one time.

The bite of a black widow spider is more dangerous than a rattlesnake.

A frog's tongue is sticky and strong.

Scorpions will eat each other.

There could be a cockroach on the moon! One is supposed to have escaped from one of the Apollo missions.

There are 6 billion dust mites in an average bed.

Botflies crash into caribou's noses spreading their m aggots, which crawl into the animal's mouth and nose to breed.

A sea urchin walks along the seabed on its teeth.

Some octopuses paralyse their prey with a poisonous bite then eat the victim while it is still alive.

The smell a squashed wasp lets off warns the rest of the nest that danger is approaching.

Parasitic wasps lay eggs inside other insects such as spiders, caterpillars and wasps.

Honeybees can recognize human faces.

The Nile Catfish swims upside down.

Dung beetles roll huge balls of dung, which they use for laying their eggs in. When the larvae hatch they munch their way out of the dung ball.

Grey whales travel distances of more than 22,000 kilometres from the arctic to Mexico annually.

Tarantula spiders flick hairs from their bodies at their prey, which causes allergic reactions.

The bird-eating spider has fangs, which inject poison and disgusting stomach juices into its prey.

Stinkbugs ooze a foul smelling liquid which predators hate and helps keep the stinkbugs safe.

The goliath bird-eating spider is a massive 28cm wide when it stretches its legs.

The carnivore dinosaurs had narrow curved, sharp teeth for tearing and ripping flesh.

One female mosquito in a year can produce over 140,000,000 young.

Sea Otters use stones to crack open shellfish.

The Filaria, a parasitic worm lives under the skin and causes boils. If you pull the worm out and it breaks it will poison you.

Only female horse flies bite before they lay eggs.

Mealy bugs ooze a sticky, white substance to protect themselves.

If you upset hornets they will chase you and give you a painful sting.

Some butterflies disguise themselves as bird droppings to save themselves from being eaten.

Soldier termites squirt a substance at their enemies, which paralyses then chokes them to death.

Insects have sharp teeth or a sting, which injects poisonous venom into their victims.

Wasps will eat each other as well as bits of other bugs.

wacky world

Your tears would not fall in space.

Wacky American place names - Beauty, KY.

The biggest snowfall was in the United States at 31.1.metres!

Unusual names - John Portsmouth Football Club Westwood

Unusual food from - South America - Guinea Pigs.

Unusual food from - Australia - Crocodile Steaks.

It takes 2 to 10 days for banana skins to decompose.

Wacky American place names - Best, TX.

Weird Fruit and Vegetables - Fat hen

Unusual food from - Brazil - Piranha Salad.

Unusual food from -
Iceland - Putrefied Shark.

It would take
3000 years to
count all the
stars in the
galaxy.

**Wacky American
place names -
Bountiful, UT.**

Wacky American place
names - Carefree, AZ.

More than 45,000
pieces of plastic
rubbish float in
every square mile
of ocean.

**The South Pole has
the least amount of
sunshine with 182
days of no sun at all.**

Unusual names - Wrigley Fields

Weird Fruit and Vegetables - Catsear

Unusual names - Bluebell Madonna Halliwell

Unusual food from -
Vietnam - Burnt Sea Slug with cashew nuts.

Wacky American place names - Celebration, FL.

The UK produces enough waste to fill Lake Windermere every 8 months.

The soggiest place on Earth is Mawsynram in India, which has rainfall of 11,873mm a year.

You have a 1 in 5 billion chance of rubbish from space falling on you.

Wacky American place names - Friendly, WV.

Unusual food from -
Vietnam - Raw fish bowels.

Weird Fruit and Vegetables - Fiddlehead

Unusual names - Baby Hospital

Unusual food from -
Kazakhstan - Smoked horse and sheep stomach.

Wacky American place names - Happyland, CT.

A litre of oil can pollute 1 million litres of fresh drinking water.

It takes an hour for a snowflake to fall to earth.

Wacky American place names - Happy Camp, CA.

One day on Pluto equals a week on earth.

Unusual food from -
China - Cold shredded jellyfish.

Weird Fruit and Vegetables - Ice Plant

Ninety percent of a plant is water.

Unusual food from -
Australia - Wichity grub soup.

Snow and ice permanently cover an eighth of the Earth's surface.

**Unusual food from -
France - Duck's gizzards.**

Unusual names -
Depressed Cupboard Cheesecake

Waste engine oil from 3 million cars in Britain remains uncollected.

Wacky American place names - Ideal, GA.

Wacky American place names - Lovely, KY.

Weird Fruit and Vegetables - Lizards tail

Weird Fruit and Vegetables - Garden Rocket

Unusual food from -
Thailand - Curried frog including head and guts.

Wacky American place
names - Magic City, ID.

The amount of cosmic
dust that falls on the
Earth every year is about
30,000 tonnes.

Unusual food from -
Ecuador - Live lemon ants.

In the UK families
throw away
between £250
and £400 worth of
edible food every
year.

Wacky American place
names - Luck Stop, KY.

Lightening strikes the Empire
State Building approximately
200 times a year.

Unusual names -
Hubert Blaine Wolfeschlegelsteinhausenbergerdorff

44,000 thunder-storms happen in the earth's atmosphere every day.

Unusual food from - China - Birds Nest Soup.

Wacky American place names - Paradise, MI.

The Great Red Spot on the planet Jupiter is a mind blowing major storm. It is 14,000 kilometres wide and 40,000 kilometres long and has been blowing for a century.

The average child before it is toilet trained uses 3,796 nappies, which end up in landfill sites.

Unusual food from - Japan - Fugu (deadly blowfish).

Wacky American place names - Smileyberg, KS.

Unusual names - Peaches Honeyblossom Michelle Charlotte Angel

Unusual names - Noddy Boffin

The coldest weather ever recorded was at Vostok Station in Antarctica, July 1983 when the temperature plummeted to -89.6 Celsius. That's cold!

Unusual food from - Saudi Arabia - Lambs eyes.

Venus twinkles in the sky like a star. It twinkles with reflected light from its deadly clouds made up of acid and dry ice.

It takes 24 trees to make 1 tonne of newspapers.

Wacky American place names - Success, MO.

Unusual food from - France - Cock's combs.

Wacky American place names - What Cheer, IA.

Weird Fruit and Vegetables - Luffa

Weird Fruit and Vegetables - Pattypan Squash

Unusual food from -
Australia - Sugar Ants.

Antofagasta in Chile
gets less than 0.1mm
of rain per year!

Wacky American place
names - Boring, OR.

Unusual food from -
South America - Iguana meat.

When it rains
on Venus it's
pouring down
sulphuric acid.

900 million items
of clothing are
sent to landfill
sites every year.

Wacky American place
names - Dinkytown, MN.

Unusual names - Mr Bumble

Unusual food from -
Africa - Fried grasshoppers.

Wacky American place names - Embarrass, WI.

Lightening bolts strike the land rather than the oceans.

A forest the size of Wales is needed every year in Britain to provide all the paper we need.

On Earth we always see the same side of the moon.

Unusual food from - Asia - Locusts.

Wacky American place names - Eek, AK.

Unusual names - Hannibal Chollop

Weird Fruit and Vegetables - Black-eyed pea

Every 90 minutes we produce enough rubbish to fill a swimming pool.

Unusual food from - France - Snails.

Wacky American place names - Flat, TX.

A pacific tropical storm called John lasted for 31 days. It changed from a hurricane to a typhoon and then back to a hurricane.

Unusual food from - China - Chicken feet.

Wacky American place names - Greasy, OK.

A moon day is equal to 27 Earth days.

Unusual names - Martin Chuzzlewit

Black pudding is blood from a pig or cow sweetened and baked.

It takes 50,000 years for a plastic container to decompose.

Wacky American place names - Gripe, AZ.

In 1986, Bangladesh was bombarded by record sized hailstones weighing over 1kg each.

The Romans ate dormice stuffed with mince.

A year on Pluto is 248 times longer than on Earth.

Wacky American place names - Hardscrabble, DE.

Unusual names - Vincent Crummles

Weird Fruit and Vegetables - Horse gram

The Romans ate wild boar stuffed with live birds, which would fly out of the stomach of the boar when cut open.

There is no air on Jupiter only hydrogen gas.

Wacky American place names - Hazard, KY.

Greenhouse gas is caused by exhaust fumes, pollution from factories and power stations, stinky methane from rubbish dumps and farting cows!

Medieval nobles ate seals.

Lightening strikes are 2 to 3 miles long. Some strikes can be 10 miles long!

Wacky American place names - Oddville, KY.

Unusual names - Mr Fezziwig

Weird Fruit and Vegetables - Winged bean

The Romans ate milk-fattened snails.

You can see lightening a 100 miles away at night!

Wacky American place names - Ordinary, KY.

You can leap much higher on the moon because you weigh six times less than on Earth.

Medieval nobles ate porpoises.

Saturn's rings are great lumps of ice, which circle the planet.

Wacky American place names - Okay, OK.

Unusual names - Mr Grimwig

Weird Fruit and Vegetables - Elephant Garlic

Wacky American place names - Peculiar, MO.

Our galaxy is called the Milky Way, yummy!

Medieval nobles ate peacocks.

There are no clouds, rain or air on the moon so don't visit without a spacesuit.

You have a 1 in 600,000 chance of being struck by lightening!

The Romans ate baked fish entrails, which they made into a sauce.

Wacky American place names - Why, AZ.

Unusual names - Uriah Heep

Weird Fruit and Vegetables - Elephant Foot Yam

Wacky American place names - Bacon, IN.

8 minutes 17 seconds is the time it takes for light to reach Earth from the Sun.

Medieval nobles ate whales.

Courtesy books at medieval feasts asked diners not to pick their nose, scratch their flea or tick bites or fart.

Ancient Greeks believed the wind was the breath of a god. Hope they didn't eat garlic!

The moon has no water so you will not need your swimming gear!

Wacky American place names - Big Rock Candy Mountain, VT.

Unusual names - Tim Likinwater

Weird Fruit and Vegetables - Pignut

The Aztec people were fond of eating dogs and armadillos.

The sun is actually a burning star.

Wacky American place names - Buttermilk, KS.

It's illegal to swear on a mini-golf course in Long Beach, California.

Comets are flying visitors from deep space made up of lumps of ice and rock.

Medieval nobles ate swans.

Wacky American place names - Cheesequake, NJ.

Unusual names - Newman Noggs

Weird Fruit and Vegetables - Sea Lettuce

The Inca people liked to feast on turkeys, dogs, wild pigs and rodents.

A meteor is a shooting star.

Wacky American place names - Chocolate Bayou, TX.

Don't go into space without a spacesuit, there is no air and it's so cold you wouldn't last long.

Medieval nobles ate herons.

You cannot own a hippopotamus in Los Angeles.

Wacky American place names - Goodfood, MS.

Unusual names - Kit Nubbles

Weird Fruit and Vegetables - Sea grape

Queen Elizabeth I loved sugar so much her teeth turned black.

There are over 800 tornadoes a year in the United States.

Wacky American place names - Ham Lake, MN.

Early English puddings were in fact made from meat and boiled in an intestine of an animal.

Wacky American place names - Hot Coffee, MS.

Uranus rotates on its side.

Donkeys cannot sleep in bathtubs in Arizona.

Unusual names - Ebenezer Scrooge

Weird Apples and Plums - Belle de Boskoop

A raindrop falls to Earth at 7 miles per hour.

Unusual food from - Sweden - Smoked Reindeer.

Wacky American place names - Lick Fork, VA.

Suspenders must not be worn in Nogales, Arizona.

Unusual food from - Laos - Water buffalo skin.

Venus is the only planet that spins backwards.

Wacky American place names - Lickskillet, OH.

Unusual names - Tilly Slowboy

Weird Apples and Plums - Catshead

Unusual food from -
Australia - Bogging moths.

Two thirds of
the earth's
surface is
covered by
water.

Wacky American place
names - Mexican Water, AZ.

At least 1000 people a year are killed by lightening.

Wacky American place
names - Oatmeal, TX.

You must not
flick snot
into the wind
in Alabama.

Unusual food from -
Australia - Honey bag bees.

Unusual names - Chevy Slyme

Weird Apples and Plums - Cockpit Improved

Unusual food from - Japan - Boiled wasp larvae.

Rubber bands last longer in the refrigerator.

Wacky American place names - Oniontown, PA.

It's illegal to park a flying saucer in any French vineyard.

Unusual food from - Japan - Fried cicadas.

Plastic takes 500 years to break down.

Wacky American place names - Picnic, FL.

Unusual names - Augustus Gloop

Weird Apples and Plums - Granny Smith

Wacky American place names - Pie Town, MN.

An olive tree can live up to 1500 years.

Unusual food from - Japan - Fried ricefield grasshoppers.

The Great Barrier Reef is the largest living structure on the planet at 2000 kilometres.

It's an offence to pawn wooden legs in Delaware.

Wacky American place names - Sandwich, MA.

Unusual food from - Japan - Fried silk moth pupae.

Unusual names - Veruca Salt

Weird Apples and Plums - King of the Pippins

Unusual food from -
Nigeria - Roasted termites.

68% of UFO
sightings are
by men.

Wacky American place
names - Spuds, FL.

It is not possible for an Astronaut to belch in space, as there is
no gravity to separate liquid from gas in the stomach.

Unusual food from -
Algeria - Locusts.

In the City of
London it is illegal
for a cab to carry
rabid dogs or
corpses.

Wacky American place
names - Sugar City, ID.

Unusual names - Violet Beauregarde

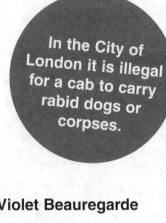

Weird Apples and Plums - Cockles Pippin

Unusual food from - Nigeria - Roasted crickets.

Wacky American place names - Tea, SD.

In Ohio, it is against the law to get a fish drunk.

There are over 1000 volcanoes that could erupt today.

Light travels in a straight line.

Unusual food from - Bali - Barbequed dragonfly.

Wacky American place names - Tortilla Flat, AZ.

Unusual names - Charlie Bucket

Weird Apples and Plums - Cornish Gilliflower

The Romans enjoyed eating herring gulls.

The Sea of Tranquility is on the moon but you can't paddle in it!

Wacky American place names - Two Egg, FL.

In London it is illegal to flag down a taxi if you have the plague.

Wacky American place names - Beebeetown, IA.

A hailstone, which weighed over 1kg fell on Bangladesh in 1986.

Roman food included such delicacies such as minced cow udders.

Unusual names - Mike Teavee

Weird Apples and Plums - Knobbed Russet

Wacky American place names - Bee Lick, KY.

It's illegal to sell your eye in Texas.

The Romans were fond of all sorts of innards from animals such as lungs, brains and

If you set off now it will take you approximately 2,000 years to walk to the sun.

Stars go on shining for 10 billion years.

Lots of people eat offal, which is usually heart, lungs, liver, tails, feet, brains and tongue.

Wacky American place names - Bird-in-Hand, PA.

Unusual names - Willy Wonka

Weird Apples and Plums - Mollie's Delicious

Wacky American place names - Birds Eye, IN.

A thousand Earth's could fit into the sun.

Recipes for offal - Braised Kidneys

In Utah it's illegal to fish from horseback.

Recipes for offal - Braised Oxtail

A bolt of lightening hitting earth is five times hotter than the sun's surface.

Wacky American place names - Black Gnat, KY.

Unusual names - Aunt Sponge

Weird Apples and Plums - Peasgood's Nonsuch

Wacky American place names - Bugscuffle, TN.

It would take you an hour driving your car straight up to reach space.

Recipes for offal - Stir-Fried Liver with cabbage

Strange Sports - Base Jumping - competitors leap off tall places such as buildings and mountains with a parachute.

Recipes for offal - Tongue and mushrooms

The sun will run out of fuel and turn into a Red Giant in 5 billion years.

Wacky American place names - Bumble Bee, AZ.

In Switzerland it's illegal to flush the toilet after 10 o clock.

Weird Fruits and Vegetables - Mangel-wurzel

Recipes for offal - Tripe and Onions

If you drop an object in the deepest ocean it would take more than an hour to hit the bottom over six miles down.

Wacky American place names - Chicken, AK.

Strange Sports - Bobsled & Skeleton Luge - competitors hurl themselves around an icy track at considerable speed.

Recipes for offal - Faggots

In relative size, if the sun were a beach ball and Jupiter a golf ball the Earth would be a pea.

Wacky American place names - Fleatown, OH.

Wacky warning labels - On a bag of peanuts - this contains nuts!

Carrots in the 18th century were purple or white.

**Recipes for offal -
Calf's Brain Soup**

The first animal
to orbit the
Earth was Laika,
a Russian dog in
1957.

Wacky American place names -
Goose Pimple Junction, VA.

Strange Sports - Bull Running in Pamplona - competitors run
through narrow streets with a number of bulls chasing them.

Wacky American place names -
Parrot, KY.

There are 336
dimples on a
golf ball.

**Recipes for offal -
Goose Liver Pate**

**Wacky warning labels -
On a hairdryer - don't use when sleeping!**

Apples keep you awake more effectively than coffee.

Recipes for offal -
Breaded Pork Trotters

Shooting stars
are meteorites
crashing through
space towards
Earth.

Wacky American place
names - Turkey, TX.

**Strange Sports - Shark Diving - The brave dive
in cages or swim free with sharks.**

Recipes for offal -
Liver Dumpling Soup

Earth is colourful
because we have
an atmosphere
and the sunlight
hitting it spreads
colour.

Wacky American place
names - Shoofly, NC.

**Wacky warning labels -
On a chainsaw - do not stop the saw with your hands!**

The pea is the oldest vegetable in the world.

Recipes for offal - Pickled Pigs Trotters

A cup of hot water freezes quicker than a cup of cold water.

Wacky American place names - Turkey Scratch, AR.

Strange Sports - Horse Racing on Ice in St Moritz, Switzerland - jockeys race around a frozen lake on horseback.

Wacky American place names - Bear, DE.

A whip cracking was the first object to break the sound barrier.

Recipes for offal - Sheep's Heart

Wacky warning labels - On an iron - do not iron clothes on body!

Honey never goes off.

Wacky American place names - Beaverdale, PA.

There is a variety of plum called a Warwickshire Drooper.

Recipes for offal - Steamed Pork Intestines

Strange Sports - Elephant Polo - teams try to score before their opponents using a standard polo ball and a very large cane.

The South Pole is in continual darkness for 182 days per year.

Wacky American place names - Dinosaur, CO.

Recipes for offal - Chitterlings (Pig Intestines) in Broth

Wacky warning labels - On a cartridge for a printer - do not eat toner!

Almonds belong to the peach family.

Wacky American place names - Dog Walk, KY.

The Ancient Romans enjoyed eating Goat Moth grubs.

Honking is cycling out of the saddle.

Strange Sports - Underwater Hockey - teams trying to score against the opposition wearing a diving mask, fins, a snorkel, a mouth guard, and using a playing glove and small stick to try and score.

Guts is a type of

An old remedy for curing deafness was hare's urine mixed with crushed earwigs.

Wacky American place names - Fish Haven, ID.

Wacky warning labels - On a baby's pram - remove child before folding!

Rice paper doesn't have any rice in it.

The Japanese enjoy worm pie.

The African baobab tree is pollinated by bats and blossoms in moonlight.

Wacky American place names - Hippo, KY.

Strange Sports - Cheese Rolling - competitors chase a 'round' of Gloucester cheese down a steep hill.

The Ancient Romans liked to eat flamingo tongues. Yummy!

Pinocchio is Italian for 'pine head'.

Wacky American place names - Horseheads, NY.

Wacky warning labels - On a rifle - misuse may cause injury!

The Eiffel Tower has 1792 steps.

Unusual food from -
China - Sun Dried Maggots

Scuba divers cannot pass wind at depths of more than 33 feet.

Wacky American place names - Hungry Horse,

Strange Sports - Zorbing - competitors hurl
down hill in a giant hamster ball.

Wacky American place names - Mammoth, WV.

In Georgia, the chicken capital of the world, it is illegal to eat chicken with a fork!

Unusual food from -
Romania - Bears Paw

Mickey Mouse was the first non-human to win an Oscar.

An average iceberg weighs 20 million tonnes.

**Unusual food from -
Turkey - Starling Stew**

Wacky American place
names - Possum Trot, KY.

**Peanuts are one of
the ingredients of
dynamite.**

**Strange Sports - Bungee Jumping - individuals jump
from a tall structure while tied to a long rubber cord.**

**Finland did not
ban Donald
Duck for not
wearing pants.**

Unusual food from -
Samoa - Baked Bats

**Wacky American place names -
Monkey's Eyebrow, KY.**

You can't breed alligators in your house in Texas.

In Connecticut there is a Nut Museum.

Unusual food from - Vietnam - Silkworm Pupae Soup

In Florida, it is not allowed to sing in a public place while wearing a swimsuit.

Wacky American place names - Rabbit Shuffle, NC.

Strange Sports - Parkour (urban running) - individuals run across the top of city landscapes.

Wacky American place names - Squirrel Hill, PA.

Cracks of 3,000 miles an hour appear when a pane of glass breaks.

Unusual food from - Philippines - Pigs organs in blood

In Texas there is a cockroach Hall of Fame museum.

1/100th of a second is called a 'jiffy'.

Delicious Tudor recipes - yummy! - Calf's foot jelly

Nine million other people share your birthday.

Wacky American place names - Toad Suck, AR.

Strange Sports - Swamp Soccer - teams play football in a swamp.

Delicious Tudor recipes - yummy! - Roast swan

In Alabama it is not allowed to wear a false moustache in church, because it may cause people to laugh.

Wacky American place names - Trout, LA.

There is a museum of Dog Collars in Kent.

A cow face is also a yoga pose.

Wacky American place names - Bigfoot, TX.

There are 100,000 tons of bubblegum chewed every year.

Delicious Tudor recipes - yummy! - Treacle tart filled with picked mackerel

Strange Sports - Indoor Sky Diving - Individual's stay in the air aided by a wind machine in a wind tunnel.

In Japan ladies cover their mouths when laughing because it's rude to show their teeth.

Wacky American place names - Viper, KY.

Delicious Tudor recipes - yummy! - Sheep's head mulled in cloves

A violin is made up of 70 pieces of wood.

The largest dinosaur eggs found weighed 7kgs.

Yellowstone National Park in the US rises 3 inches every year due to a volcano underneath it.

Delicious Tudor recipes - yummy! - Boiled pigeon

Wacky American place names - Bowlegs, OK.

Strange Sports - Shin Kicking - competitors try to kick each other's shins. Steel capped boots are now banned.

Delicious Tudor recipes - yummy! - Calf's lungs

An island made up entirely of rubbish has been discovered in the Pacific Ocean. It weighs approximately three million tons.

Wacky American place names - Brainy Boro, NJ.

In Sweden the law states it is illegal for parents to insult their children.

The sun is 300,000 times bigger than the Earth!

Wacky American place names - Humansville, MO.

It's not allowed in Alabama to carry an ice-cream cone in your back pocket.

Delicious Tudor recipes - yummy! - Meat custard

Strange Sports - Kabaddi - competitors hold their breath and try and wrestle the opposition.

Delicious Regency recipes - yummy! - Ox tongue

Texas is the only state where you can cast a vote from space.

Wacky American place names - Left Hand, WV.

The route to the top of Mount Everest is covered in rubbish and the bodies of over 120 climbers who didn't make it.

The Earth travels through space at 530km a second.

Delicious Regency recipes - yummy! - Coffin Pie, a huge heavy pastry pie with a lid filled with (sheep's tongues, bone marrow, check, veal, pigeon breast, oysters and nutmeg)

A ten-gallon hat only holds three-quarters of a gallon!

Wacky American place names - Shoulderblade, KY.

Strange Sports - Bossaball - competitors play volleyball but on trampolines.

Delicious Victorian recipes - yummy! - Layered Pie (a variety of over 20 different carcasses)!

In Russia it is an offence to drive around in a dirty car.

Wacky American place names - Stiffknee Knob,

Strange City Names - Archangel - Russia

Ketchup was sold in the 1820's as medicine.

Delicious Regency recipes - yummy! - Cheese with the maggots that live on it!

There is a Fairy Investigation Society.

Wacky American place names - Sweet Lips, TN.

Strange Sports - Bog Snorkelling - competitors have to complete lengths of a trench cut through a peat bog wearing a snorkel and flippers.

Wacky American place names - West Thumb, WY.

Light hitting our planet Earth now is 30 thousand years old.

The Vikings ate seagull stew.

Strange City Names - Bandung - Indonesia

The yo-yo was originally a weapon used in the Philippines.

Octopuses are eaten in Spain cooked in their own ink.

You can arrange 10 books on a shelf 3,628,800 different ways.

Wacky American place names - Blow Me Down, Canada.

Olympic Sports that are no longer played - Standing High Jump.

Wacky American place names - Ding Dong, TX.

The month of October was designated as National Pizza Month starting in 1987.

During hard times Viking bread contained peas, flour and tree bark from pine trees.

Strange City Names - Bogota - Colombia

High jumping headfirst and landing on your back is called the Fosbury Flop.

Vikings ate whale meat and blubber.

The International Vinegar Festival is held every June in Roslyn, South Dakota.

Wacky American place names - Looneyville, TX.

Olympic Sports that are no longer played - Standing Broad Jump.

In Japan raw squid is eaten with soy sauce.

The Universe was the size of a pea one million, million, million, million, millionth of a second after the Big Bang.

Wacky British place names - Bacon End

Strange City Names - Buffalo - USA

March 14th is Potato Chip Day!

The Roman Emperor Vitellus was fond of eating pheasant brain and flamingo tongues.

The Moon, Sun and Earth are all 4.56 billion years old!

Wacky British place names - Beacon's Bottom

Olympic Sports that are no longer played - Standing Hop, Step, Jump.

In Japan you can have ox tongue flavoured ice cream.

Immersing a chicken bone in vinegar for 24 hours will make it rubbery.

Wacky British place names - Barton in the Beans

Strange City Names - Chihuahua - Mexico

The biggest galaxies have a million, million stars!

Wacky British place names -
Bottoms

Sausages were called
bangers during the
Second World War
because they contained
so much water they
exploded when fried.

In Italy cuttlefish are
cooked in their own ink.

Olympic Sports that are no longer played -
16lb Shot Put with two hands.

From the Star War
movie the Empire
Strikes Back one
of the asteroids in
the famous scene
is a potato.

Wacky Pudding Names -
Spotted Dick

Wacky British place names -
Bogend

Strange City Names -Chittagong - Bangladesh

There are 100 billion galaxies in the Universe!

When rhubarb is used in hair dye it produces the shade blond. The active ingredient is chrysophanol.

Wacky Pudding Names - Trifle

Wacky British place names - Buttock's Booth

Olympic Sports that are no longer played - Stone Throw.

Wacky British place names - Great Snoring

Blibber-Blubber was introduced in 1906 and it is called Bubblegum today.

Wacky Pudding Names - Sticky Toffee Pudding

Strange City Names - Cracow - Poland

Bagpipes are mentioned in the bible.

Wacky Pudding Names - Hasty Pudding

More energy is emitted by Quasars than 100 giant galaxies.

Wacky British place names - Knockin

Olympic Sports that are no longer played - Discus with two hands.

Wacky Pudding Names - Bread and Butter Pudding

Ping Pong balls can travel 106 miles per hour!

Wacky British place names - Lickey End

Strange City Names - Dandong - China

The Battle of Hastings took place in Battle.

Wacky Pudding Names - Roly-poly

The Universe gets bigger by a billion miles every hour.

Wacky British place names - Middle Wallop

Olympic Sports that are no longer played - Javelin with two hands.

Wacky Pudding Names - Lardy Cake

A trillion has 12 zeros and a googol has 100 zeros.

Wacky British place names - Mucking

Strange City Names - El Giza - Egypt

31,536,000 seconds make up a year!

**Wacky Pies -
Steak and Kidney pie**

**Coca Cola
was green
when it was
first
produced.**

Wacky British place names -
Nettlebed

Olympic Sports that are no longer played - Tug-of-War.

Wacky Pies -
Stargaze Pie (herrings cooked in a
pie with their heads looking out)

**French Fries
are originally
from Belgium
not France.**

**Wacky British place names -
Ramsbottom**

Strange City Names - Fez - Morocco

66,000 Crème Eggs are made every hour.

Wacky Pies -
Black Pudding (onions, pork fat,
cereal and blood)

There are
170,000,000,000,000,
000.000,000,000
ways to play ten
opening moves
in chess.

Wacky British place names -
Steeple Bumpstead

Olympic Sports that are no longer played - Club Swinging.

Sailors took hot cross buns to
sea to prevent a shipwreck.

Liquorice was
found in King
Tut's tomb.

Wacky British place names -
Lower Slaughter

Strange City Names - Funabashi - Japan

Candy floss is 100% sugar.

Sushi is a raw fish dish.

One million earthquakes shake the Earth every year.

Wacky British place names - Steeple-on-Rule

Olympic Sports that are no longer played - Tumbling.

Wacky British place names - Nitshill

A 3 metre high Easter egg was constructed in Australia.

In Transylvania they have stuffed cabbage for Christmas dinner.

Strange City Names - Gorky - Russia

100 lightening bolts strike the Earth every second.

Australia has its Christmas holiday in the middle of summer.

The Swedes have baked ham, pickled herring, lutfish and rice pudding for Christmas dinner.

Wacky British place names - Boghead

Olympic Sports that are no longer played - Underwater swimming.

Wacky British place names - Shellow Bowells

74% of children eat the ears on chocolate bunnies first.

A normal person disposes of 74kg of organic waste every year.

Strange City Names - Kathmandu - Nepal

There are approximately 1,150 windmills that still work in the Netherlands.

It takes 500 to 800 years for nappies to decompose.

Seven billion pounds of chocolate and candy are manufactured in the US each year.

Wacky British place names - Splatt

Olympic Sports that are no longer played - Obstacle race in the pool.

The world's biggest ice-cream cake was made in China in 2006. It was 4.8 metres long, 3 metres wide, 1 metre high and weighed 8 tons.

Wacky British place names - Thong

8 tonnes of rubbish is thrown away everyday in England and Wales.

Strange City Names - Mysore - India

25 recycled drink bottles can make one fleece jacket.

There are more mobile telephones in the UK than people.

Every seven weeks a person in the UK throws away his or her own body weight in rubbish.

Wacky British place names - Wyre Piddle

Olympic Sports that are no longer played - Weightlifting - One handed.

If you went for a space walk without a suit you would explode before you died of suffocation.

A cake, which weighed 58 tons was made by the people of Fort Payne, Alabama in 1989.

Wacky British place names - Ugley

Strange City Names - Ningbo - China

Britain uses 15 million plastic bottles a day.

The first ice skates were made from animal bones.

The longest beard has been recorded at 5.33 metres.

Wacky British place names - Pratt's Bottom

Olympic Sports that are no longer played - All Round Dumbbell Contest.

Bare-knuckle fighting - a gruesome sport from the past where two fighters fought each other with bare knuckles.

Some lipstick contains a tiny amount of fish scales.

The favourite toy for kids in 1900 was plasticine.

Strange City Names - Pingxiang - China

An apple pip contains cyanide!

Bull/Bear-baiting - a gruesome sport from the past where dogs were set on bulls and bears in pits.

It is claimed that the average bar of chocolate has eight insect legs in it.

The dot over the letter i is called a tittle.

Olympic Sports that are no longer played - Shooting with Duelling Pistol.

Strange Sports - World Nettle Eating Championship - UK

300 million square metres of land are filled with rubbish every year. That much rubbish would cover the pitch of Manchester United FC 28,450 times.

Ringing bells are supposed to drive away the undead.

Strange City Names - Zigong - China

Comets are made up of dust and ice, which makes them grimy snowballs.

6 billion aluminium cans are used every year in the UK. This many cans can make a pathway to the moon and back.

The Stinkhorn fungus smells disgusting to attract flies.

Olympic Sports that are no longer played - Live Pigeon Shooting.

Strange Sports - World Gurning (pulling silly faces) Championship - UK

If you take any number, double it, add 10, divide it by 2, subtract the number you started with, the answer will always be 5.

Cock fighting - a gruesome sport from the past where two cockerels with sharp spurs on their feet would fight each other.

Many airports around the world have no gate 13!

spooky

It's bad luck to milk a cow that's going to market.

Creepy gargoyles on medieval buildings are to ward off evil spirits.

If rats leave a ship it will sink.

The Beast of Exmoor is a large black cat similar to a puma or panther that roams the moor.

Panophobia - Fear of everything.

Abraham Lincoln is supposed to haunt the White House.

Basilisk was a snake and looking at it would kill you

Oliver Cromwell's ghost is said to haunt his house in Ely.

Lachanophobia - Fear of vegetables.

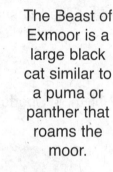

Knocking on wood brings good luck.

Anne Boleyn the beheaded wife of King Henry VIII is said to wander and haunt the Tower of London with her head tucked under her arm. Two more of his wives haunt the corridors of Hampton Court Palace.

The spirits of Sir Walter Raleigh and Guy Fawkes are said to haunt the Tower of London.

Pogonophobia - Fear of beards.

It's bad luck to mention the Scottish play 'Macbeth'.

Ichthyophobia - Fear of fish.

Legends say that werewolves were people who had made a pact with the devil.

If you sneeze three times before breakfast it's good luck.

Nessie the Loch Ness Monster is a creature that is supposed to live in Loch Ness in Scotland. Nessie is supposed to look like an extinct dinosaur called a plesiosaur.

Spring Heeled Jack was a ghost that roamed London in Victorian Times. Some people said he looked like the devil, had claws, could breathe flames and had eyes of fire. His legend did not die out; he was spotted many times in the 20th century.

Mary Queen of Scots, who had her head chopped off, is supposed to haunt many castles and houses including Stirling Castle.

Old wives tales and superstition - The dried body of a frog worn in a bag around the neck stops a person having fits.

The Bermuda Triangle also called the Devils Triangle is an area where aircraft and ships just disappear. In the past 30 years, over 100 ships and aeroplanes have been lost and over 1,000 people have disappeared.

Sophophobia - Fear of learning.

Actors never say good luck they say 'break a leg.'

Alektorophobia - Fear of chickens.

An apple a day keeps the doctor away.

Three butterflies together is good luck.

Ablutophobia -
Fear of washing.

A black cat crossing your path is good luck.

Florence Nightingale is supposed to haunt St.Thomas's Hospital in London. She's probably still making sure everything is nice and clean!

Pengersick Castle in Cornwall is a very haunted castle. Twenty ghosts are supposed to haunt the castle including a young girl who was blown off the battlements in medieval times. She attempts to blow visitors of the battlements today.

Linonophobia -
Fear of string.

Jamaica Inn in Cornwall has a ghost of a murdered sailor who is seen wandering around.

Black Dogs in folklore are said to be bad omens. Sightings of strange black dogs are still made today.

Saying white rabbits on the first day of each new month brings good luck.

Medusa was a gorgon with snakes for hair and her stare turned you to stone.

Ghosts often do not know they are dead.

Big Foot or Sasquatch is a creature between seven to ten feet tall, covered in hair and smells like a skunk or dead animal. Many people over the centuries claim to have seen it.

It's unlucky to walk under a ladder.

The Mary Celeste was a sailing ship, which was found abandoned and adrift in 1872 close to the Azores. There was no sign of life or any bodies.

If you break a mirror it's seven years bad luck.

It's unlucky to see one magpie.

Old wives tales and superstition - If you pick your nose your finger will stick up there.

Arachnephobia - Fear of spiders.

Blennophobia - Fear of slime.

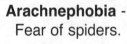

Ghosts can appear to the living in dreams.

The Dolphin Inn, Penzance is haunted by an old sea captain who was hanged by the infamous 'Hanging' Judge Jeffries.

It's bad luck to open an umbrella inside.

Dark, smoky ghostly figures are dark entities which you should be wary of. They can appear at the foot of a bed.

Spilling salt is bad luck so throw a little over your shoulder.

Bromidrosiphobia - Fear of body smells.

Bogyphobia - Fear of bogeys or the bogeyman.

In Washington, the Capital Building is supposed to be haunted by a demonic cat.

It's bad luck to put new shoes on the table.

It's bad luck to pass anyone on the stairs.

A phantom female hitchhiker is reportedly seen at Blue Bell Hill in Kent.

Coprophobia - Fear of faeces.

Minotaur was half bull and half man, which lived in a maze and killed people.

If the ravens leave the Tower of London the crown will be lost.

The museum at RAF Cosford is haunted by the ghost of an aircraft engineer.

There are certain places called portals where ghosts are transported from their world to our.

Emetophobia - Fear of vomiting.

Kraken was a giant sea monster, which attacked ships and ate the crew.

Noisy ghosts are called poltergeists.

A ghostly monk and a young woman who was murdered roam the corridors of Chingle Hall, near Goosnargh, Preston.

If you have an itchy nose you are going to have an argument.

If you see a dog eating grass it will rain.

London's Old Bailey criminal court has a ghost that appears when important trials are being held.

The ghost of a roman soldier is seen on Easter Day near the village of Bayston in Shropshire.

Herpetophobia - Fear of creepy crawlies.

Ommetaphobia - Fear of eyeballs.

Tie a knot in your handkerchief to frighten off evil.

Animals can sense spirits and ghosts.

Lady Dorothy Southworth locally known as the 'White Lady' haunts Salmsbury Hall, Lancashire. She wanders about weeping.

Hydra was a serpent with nine heads that grew a new head every time one was cut off.

Windsor Castle is haunted by a number of ghosts including Anne Boleyn and her daughter Elizabeth I.

It's bad luck to kill a ladybird.

Pediculophobia - Fear of lice.

Brides need something old, something new, something borrowed, something blue on their wedding day.

Hang a horseshoe in your bedroom to keep nightmares away.

Scoleciphobia - Fear of worms.

It's good luck to find a four-leaf clover.

Mutiny House, New Delhi, India has ghosts of British soldiers some of them with missing limbs moving around at dusk.

Bibliophiles love books.

Edinburgh Castle in Scotland has a ghostly drummer boy and a piper.

Ophiophiles love snakes.

The early Egyptians believed in ghosts.

St Joseph of Cupertino - is the patron saint of Astronauts.

Old wives tales and superstition - catch a falling autumn leaf and you won't have a winter cold!

Harpy was a bird with a face of a woman, which carried people to hell.

Consecotaleophobia is the fear of chopsticks.

Mythical vampires are supposed to cheat death by sucking the blood of humans.

A ghostly climber has been seen on Mount Everest.

Ghosts are believed to not to be able to cross water.

The most haunted house in London is supposed to be 50 Berkeley Square.

In Belgium it is rude to talk to someone with your hands in your pockets.

St Vitus is the patron saint of dancers.

Turophiles love cheese.

Ghostly soldiers are often seen doing battle at Edgehill usually on October 23rd.